THE SAGA BEGINS

The Saga Begins

STAN CAMPBELL

VICTOR BOOKS®

A DIVISION OF SCRIPTURE PRESS PUBLICATIONS INC.
USA CANADA ENGLAND

BibleLog Series

The Saga Begins
That's the Way the Kingdom Crumbles
Fighters and Writers
What's This World Coming To?
Jesus: God Undercover
Growing Pains: The Church Hits the Road
From the Desk of the Apostle Paul
The Saga Never Ends

BibleLog is an inductive Bible study series for high school students. This eight-book series takes you through the Bible in two years if you study one chapter each week. You may want to use BibleLog in your daily devotions, completing a chapter a week by working through a few pages each day. This book is also designed to be used in group study. A leader's guide with visual aids (reproducible student sheets) is available for each book from your local Christian bookstore or from the publisher.

6   7   8   9   10   Printing/Year   94   93

Scripture taken from the *Holy Bible, New International Version,* © 1973, 1978, 1984, International Bible Society. Used by permission of Zondervan Bible Publishers.

Cover illustration and interior illustrations: John Hawk

Library of Congress Catalog Card Number: 87-62499
ISBN: 0-89693-656-2

Recommended Dewey Decimal Classification: 248.83
Suggested Subject Heading: YOUTH—RELIGIOUS LIFE

CONTENTS

INTRODUCTION

WHY ANOTHER BIBLE STUDY SERIES?

Countless thousands of young people have, at some point in their lives, decided to read through the Bible. Pastors, youth leaders, parents, or peers have preached the benefits of, "Read your Bible," "Get into the Word," "Meditate on Scripture," and so forth. And after hearing so many worthwhile challenges, a lot of determined, committed kids of ages past have dusted off the covers of their Bibles and set themselves to the task ahead.

They usually make a noble effort too. Genesis whizzes past before they know it. *("Hey, this Bible study stuff isn't so bad!")* Exodus isn't quite as fast-paced but it has its strong points. *("OK. I'm hanging in there. Two books down; 64 to go!")* Then comes Leviticus. *("I've been doin' pretty good lately. Maybe I'll take a week or so off.")* Then Numbers and Deuteronomy. *("Hey, man, who cares how long it takes to purify a healed leper?")* In most cases, the first five books of the Bible are enough to do in even the most eager readers. And instead of feeling like they've accomplished something, all those people feel is guilt because they didn't finish what they started.

That's why this Bible study series was developed. It calls for a one-year commitment on your part to get through the Old Testament. By following the session plans we provide for you, you need to complete only one session each week to accomplish your one-year goal. You won't read the entire Old Testament word for word (we'll zip you through some of the longer passages of law, prophecy, etc.), but you *will* go much more in-depth than most of the Old Testament overviews you may have tried. You will still be challenged just to get through the major flow of Old Testament action in one year.

WHAT MAKES THIS BIBLE STUDY DIFFERENT?

Here are some distinctives of this Bible study series:

- *This series is inductive.* In plain English, all that means is that we don't try to shove a lot of information down your throat. We provide the Scripture references and let you discover the content for yourself. An inductive study allows God to speak to you directly instead of having someone else interpret the material for you.

- *This series is interactive.* The purpose is not just to cover the main events of the Old Testament so you will know what happened a few thousand years ago. Each session concludes with a "Journey Inward" section, giving you an opportunity to apply any spiritual lessons you discover in the session to your own life. It might be tempting to skip these sections, or to zip through them hurriedly and with little thought. But no Bible study is complete until you put into practice what you have learned.

- *This series is youth-oriented.* A study of the content of the Old Testament will be beneficial to any age-group, of course. But BibleLog books are directed to young people.

- *This series is adaptable.* While we recommend one session per week on the average, you can study at your own pace. Go faster if you want to. (No one says you *have* to finish the series in one year if you want to go slower and let the content sink in.)

- *This series is open, direct, and complete.* It doesn't skip the "sensitive" parts of the Bible and will deal with content you never heard in Sunday School. The Old Testament contains graphic and "adult" accounts of murder, rape, incest, homosexuality, family hatred, prostitution, and other horrible sins. This series won't skip over these topics, because the same problems exist today. They are recorded in the Bible for a purpose, and we should learn from these negative illustrations as well as the many positive ones.

HOW TO GET THE MOST OUT OF THIS SERIES

We recommend a group study for this series, if possible. If group members work through the sessions individually during the week, the time your group needs to spend going over *facts* will be greatly reduced. With the content portion completed prior to the group meeting, your group time can emphasize the *application* of the biblical concepts to your individual members. (A leader's guide is available to direct your group in a review of the content. But the real strength of the leader's guide is to show you how to apply what you are learning.) If you don't have the opportunity to go through this series with a group, that's OK too. Just be sure to think through all of the "Journey Inward" sections at the end of each session. And if you have questions about what you are studying, most pastors or adult Christians you know will be more than happy to help you.

A glance at the "Snapshots" section in each session will help you remember major events and people. It also gives you a key verse to memorize if you wish.

This series is based on the *New International Version* of the Bible, so we recommend that you use it to complete the questions. If you're using another translation, the wording will differ somewhat.

WHAT TO LOOK FOR IN BOOK 1

As you work through this first book in the BibleLog series, expect to see a lot of *contrasts*. One you can't miss is God's love and perfection contrasted with mankind's sinfulness and disobedience. Second, the Old Testament heroes and heroines, even with their many shortcomings, stand in bold contrast to the many wicked men you will read about. A third contrast to look for is in the results of choices. When a character chooses to do what God wants him or her to do, keep your eyes open for what happens to that character. Contrast that person's life with a character who chooses *not* to do what God has instructed. Finally, look for comparisons and contrasts in *your* life and the lives of these Old Testament characters—both the good ones and the bad ones.

Here's a challenge to get you started, taken from the section of the Old Testament you are about to study.

"Do not let this Book of the Law depart from your mouth; meditate on it day and night, so that you may be careful to do everything written in it. Then you will be prosperous and successful" (Joshua 1:8).

A PERFECT BEGINNING; A FATAL MISTAKE

(Genesis 1–5)

New things usually generate excitement. It's amusing to see how a new baby can instantly turn a full-grown, supposedly mature adult into a strange, goo-goo-eyed creature who can speak only nonsense syllables. And the anticipation of a new car can produce saintly behavior from what was an ordinary teenager just last week. Lawns get mowed, chores get done, and rooms (that could be declared archeological digs) get cleaned—all within 20 minutes of hearing a parent say, "Since you're 16 now and have your license, I think it's time you had your own. . . . " Even a new year gets people excited. Just watch the hordes of humanity at Times Square at 11:59 P.M. any New Year's Eve, ready to celebrate one "new" day as opposed to the other 364.

New experiences put most people through a flurry of emotions. The move from junior high to high school can evoke anticipation, satisfaction, and joy. But it can also result in degrees of fear, uncertainty, and social discomfort. Learning to drive and getting a license is a thrill, but the first time you get turned around in a big city or have a "near miss" with another vehicle is a frightening sensation. So even the best new experiences can have unpleasant side effects.

As you read this page, you are beginning a new book—possibly a new commitment to Bible study as well. Before you read any farther, stop for a moment to analyze how you feel about starting this new project.

It may be natural for you to approach a study of the Bible with the attitude, *Oh, no. This is going to be a big bore.* And if that's your approach, you may be right. The success of any study of this kind depends on the attitude of the learner. And sure, you have probably had some less-than-thrilling experiences with Sunday School and/or Bible study in the past. Most of us have.

But if you approach it with an open mind, the Old Testament is as current as tomorrow's newspaper. You won't even get out of Genesis until you have dealt with topics such as broken families, betrayal by friends, homosexuality, incest, rape, murder, greed, and much more. And you may be surprised to see how many of *your* problems you recognize in the lives of these Old Testament characters.

As you begin your trek through the Bible, you will soon discover that the Book of Genesis is full of new beginnings—of the world, mankind, families, sin, society, languages, etc. It won't take long for you to realize the disastrous effects of the sin of Adam and Eve on God's perfect world, but you will also see the beginning of God's plan to redeem mankind.

When you begin reading Genesis, one question is likely to come to mind right away: How is it possible for anyone to write about the beginning of the world when the only person around was God?

It is generally accepted that Moses wrote the first five books of the Bible under the inspiration of God—possibly while the Israelites wandered through the desert for 40 years (see session 9 for more on that story). Since God felt it was important for mankind to know about the origins of life on our planet, let's take a look at the record He has given us.

 JOURNEY ONWARD

Read Genesis 1:1–2:3. As you do, use the space below to write down what God created on each day. Also record any comments or questions that come up while you read.

Day 1—(1:3-5)

Day 2—(1:6-8)

Day 3—(1:9-13)

Day 4—(1:14-19)

Day 5—(1:20-23)

Day 6—(1:24-31)

Day 7—(2:1-3)

When you think about it, God could have created only one kind of bird, one kind of fish, one animal, one tree, one flower, etc. Why do you think He chose to make such a variety of species?

Did you notice anything significant about the reference to God in Genesis 1:26? If so, what did you discover about God from that verse?

Genesis 2:4-25 provides a flashback with more information about how God created man (and woman). This passage also gives several specifics to help us better understand the location and events surrounding creation. As you read through these verses, answer the questions below.

God formed the animals out of the ground (2:19), and He also formed man out of the dust of the ground (2:7). So what is it that makes man any more special than the other animals? (You may need to refer back to 1:27.)

What were some of man's responsibilities in the garden? (1:28; 2:8, 15, 19)

What two trees were in the garden, and what restriction was placed on one of the trees? (2:9, 16-17)

Why and how was woman created? (2:20-25)

Reread Genesis 2:24. If you've been to many weddings, you have probably heard this verse read frequently. But notice its location here in Genesis. God has just established His model for love and marriage—one man and one woman who can unite physically and emotionally and become one person. God makes it clear that for this reason a man should leave his father and mother to support his wife. Think about that statement for a moment. Adam and Eve didn't have a human father or mother. But even at this point, God wanted to establish a standard for future generations to follow.

God made sure that everything was perfect "in the beginning." He created a perfect world and left it in charge of His most outstanding creations—man and woman. The story of what happened then (Genesis 3) is a familiar one, but let's reexamine some of the details.

SNEAKY SERPENT

When Satan (working through the serpent) was trying to deceive the woman (Eve), he used a variety of tricks. The first thing he did was to get Eve to question what she had been told. Of all the trees in the expanse of the Garden of Eden, God's instructions were to not eat from *one* of them. But Satan asked Eve, "Did God really say, 'You must not eat from *any* tree in the garden'?" (3:1) God had created a world and handed it over to Adam and Eve, and immediately Satan began to try to get them to question God's goodness.

Eve's reply to the serpent was not exactly truthful. Compare God's instructions to Adam (2:16-17) with Eve's reply to the serpent (3:2-3). How did Eve's answer differ from what God had really said?

The next trick Satan used was a half-truth. What did he tell Eve? (3:4-5)

How was Satan's answer true? How was it a lie?

Where was Adam while Satan's temptation of Eve was taking place? (3:6)

Eve usually takes a lot of blame for eating the forbidden fruit, but if you examine the account closely, you will see that Adam is just as guilty (perhaps more so). While Eve was tempted directly by Satan to sin, Adam appears to go along with it just on the urging of his wife. Eve also had what she thought were some pretty good reasons for eating the fruit. What were they? (3:6)

Eve's "logical" reasoning led to her sin. Satan is a master deceiver because he seems to use logic. But his logic is faulty. It simply is not logical to do something God has said not to do, because God always knows what is best for us.

Satan was right about Adam and Eve being able to distinguish good from evil (3:22), but he gave no hint of the consequences they would face for their action. What were the immediate results of Adam and Eve's sin? (3:7-13) How did their action affect their relationship with God and with each other?

What were the long-range consequences of this sin:

● For the serpent? (3:14-15)

- For women? (3:16)

- For men? (3:17-19)

After their sin, why weren't Adam and Eve allowed to remain in the Garden of Eden? (3:22-24)

Notice that God made garments of skin for Adam and Eve to wear after they became aware of their nakedness (3:21). Man's attempt to cover his own sin (3:7) was not adequate. Fig leaves may have seemed sufficient at first, but they were a very temporary solution. In autumn, when the leaves would begin to fall, Adam and Eve would be left with the same problem. Fig leaves provided a feeble alternative to animal skins.

Yet notice also that God's provision was more costly than Adam and Eve's. The animals used to make clothing for Adam and Eve were the first things that we know of to die (physically) in the Bible. Blood had to be shed because of sin. As we go on through our study of the Old Testament, the emphasis on blood sacrifices will become much stronger. In fact, the issue of sacrifice came up soon after Adam and Eve were evicted from the Garden of Eden.

BROTHER AGAINST BROTHER

Read Genesis 4:1-9. Why do you think God accepted Abel's offering and not Cain's? (You may want to consult Hebrews 11:4 and 1 John 3:12 for hints.)

Why do you think Cain murdered Abel? (Remember that this is the first murder in the history of the world. Cain acted on his own and not in imitation of anything he had seen.) What other options did Cain have?

Read Genesis 4:10-16. Do you think God's punishment of Cain was too severe? Why or why not?

Apparently the earth at this time was being populated rapidly. Some people wonder where Cain's wife came from (4:17) since the only people named so far have been Adam, Eve, Cain, and Abel. One explanation is the possibility that Adam and Eve had children while still in the Garden of Eden. Since God's judgment on the woman was to "greatly increase your pains in childbearing" (3:16), perhaps Eve had already experienced childbirth *without* pain. No one knows for sure how long they were there before being forced to leave. It is possible that many generations may have passed by the time Cain and Abel were born. Consequently, Cain could have chosen a wife who was not closely related to him. (But no one knows for sure.)

The spread of mankind on earth is described in Genesis 4:17-26. Read the passage and answer the following questions.

Who was the first city builder? (If there was a city, there *must* have been a lot of people.)

Who was the first bigamist (a person with more than one husband or wife)?

Who was the first musician?

Who pioneered metal tools?

Genesis 5 lists the major people in the family tree of Adam (through Noah). Two people stand out (for different reasons): Enoch and Methuselah. Why was Enoch special? (5:21-24)

Why was Methuselah special? (5:25-27)

 JOURNEY INWARD

Based on what you learned in this session, spend a little time thinking about **relationships between people and God.** Imagine the earth before creation—as barren as the other planets in our solar system are now. But when God decided to touch it, the earth responded in a miraculous and wonderful way. Human lives need to undergo similar changes.

If you ever feel "formless and empty," perhaps all you need is the presence of God in your life. Just as the earth survives as long as it rotates around the sun, human beings function best when God is at the center of their lives. (If you've never asked God into your life, or if you've been out of fellowship with Him for a while, you'll get a lot more out of this series if you take time *now* to confess your sins and receive His forgiveness.)

If, like Adam and Eve, you have committed a sin in direct disobedience to God's commands, He can forgive you.

If, like Abel, you are persecuted for no good reason, God is still in control of the situation.

If, like Cain, there is jealousy or hatred in your family, you can ask God for help before the circumstances get even worse.

If you are facing temptations that seem impossible to overcome, God's strength and wisdom can get you through—as long as you don't give up and take the matter into your own hands.

If, like Enoch, you walk with God, He will lead you faithfully and give you peace in any situation.

Did you notice the unmarred relationship between God and mankind that *God* established? God created a world full of beauty, peace, and variety. He then created two human beings—in His own image—and put them in charge of that perfect world. Adam and Eve were naked, yet they were innocent. (Their nakedness did not result in embarrassment, giggles, or dirty jokes, like similar situations would today.) And God, in some form, would walk through the garden and talk with them.

You see, *God* wants close fellowship with His human creations. It was *man* who broke off the relationship that God had established. Yet there is a tendency to blame God for occasionally seeming to be distant. Perhaps you've heard other people say that God doesn't seem very close on a particular day (as if God is weaving in and out of their reach).

Now a question for you to think about: If God wanted to be so close to Adam and Eve, why did He put the tree of the knowledge of good and evil in the garden and tell them not to eat of its fruit?

The Bible states clearly that God does not tempt people (James 1:13), so that can't be the answer to the previous question. But the very next verse explains that people *can* be tempted by their own evil desires (James 1:14-15). What desire do you think Adam and Eve had in mind when they ate the fruit from the tree of the knowledge of good and evil?

The problem arose when Adam and Eve had to choose between obedience to God and acting to satisfy their own desires. Do you think God was unfair to give them that choice? Or did He give them free choice for a good reason? Explain your answers.

Now how about you? What desires do you have that could possibly come into opposition with God's will for your life? Make a list of them below (or at least in your head). Keep your list in mind as you work through the following sessions in this book. Hopefully, you will discover some specific things you can do to let God work in your life to either resolve your conflicts or give you the wisdom and patience to live with them.

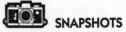 **SNAPSHOTS**

Remember today's travels with this look backward.

Creation: God created the heavens and the earth and all its inhabitants, including people. God was pleased with His creation—especially man, who was created in God's image. Adam and Eve were told to multiply and rule the earth.

The Fall: God allowed Adam and Eve to choose whether to obey Him. When they disobeyed, pain, hardship and, ultimately, death entered their lives and the human race. Because of sin, man is separated from God and needs to be reconciled to Him.

Key Verse: "So God created man in His own image, in the image of God He created him; male and female He created them" (Genesis 1:27).

Etc.: (Your own questions, comments, observations)

RAIN, RAIN, GO AWAY

(Genesis 6–11)

How do you respond when you hear of unusual occurrences of nature taking place in your area? Let's say your TV weatherperson forecasts a meteor shower or comet to come streaming through the skies the next night. Do you plan to get away from the city lights so you can get a good view? Do you give a halfhearted glance upward if you happen to be outside anyway? Or do you stay inside and watch *Gilligan's Island* reruns on TV?

Everybody seems to have some degree of interest in the out-of-the-ordinary or unexplained. If a teacher at school has six toes on each foot, everyone seems to know about it before the second day of school has begun. Think of how much of your conversation centers around whose clothes or hairstyles are most unusual. And books and TV shows like *Ripley's Believe It or Not* have kept people fascinated for years.

Yet there's a tremendous difference between showing a little interest in an unusual event that has been predicted and actually taking action on what you know. Every year you hear about people who die or are seriously injured because they stayed in an area where a tornado or flood had been predicted, yet they disregarded the information. This session covers a biblical example of a similar occurrence.

The last session referred briefly to the way people respond to *new* situations. Adam and Eve had the best new things that God could offer, yet they wound up sweating outside the Garden of Eden trying to make a living. This session picks up a few years later and deals with how people reacted to an *unusual* event that was prophesied to occur. The earth is more populated as this session begins, but most of the people have forgotten all about God and have begun to do as they please.

But before moving to the main story of this session, let's take a minute to address several references in Genesis 6:1-4 that may be somewhat unclear. For instance:

- **The sons of God** (6:2)—Some people have suggested that this phrase refers to the descendants of Seth (God's replacement for Abel). Others think perhaps it refers to kings who were ruling at the time. But many Bible scholars think "the sons of God" were angels who had joined in Satan's rebellion against God and had been thrown out of heaven. Even though angels weren't intended to marry or participate in reproduction (Mark 12:25), this group sinned and bore human offspring. Perhaps these angels are the ones referred to in Jude 6 who were imprisoned by God because they "did not keep their positions of authority but abandoned their own home." (More about angels in human form in the next session.)

- **The Nephilim** (6:4)—This name was derived from a Hebrew word meaning "to fall," revealing that the Nephilim were powerful men who would fall on others. (In the *King James Version* they are referred to as "giants.") The verse suggests that the Nephilim were already on the earth before the marriages of the "sons of God" referred to in

Genesis 6:2. The only other biblical reference to the Nephilim is in Numbers 13:33, which reaffirms that they were large and strong people.

● The meaning of Genesis 6:3 is also difficult to define precisely. The reference to 120 years may indicate God's intent to shorten man's life span (which took place after the flood) or a warning that the flood would occur in 120 years.

JOURNEY ONWARD

But regardless of any confusion you might have after reading Genesis 6:1-4, the next section is very clear. Read Genesis 6:5-13 and answer the following questions.

In the last session you saw that Adam and Eve chose to eat of the fruit of the tree of the knowledge of good and evil. What was the eventual outcome of being able to differentiate good from evil? (6:5)

How was Noah different from the rest of the people during his time? (6:8-10)

Read Genesis 6:11-18. In the space below, draw a picture of the ark. Keep it proportionate as much as possible. (If your Bible gives the measurements in cubits, keep in mind that one cubit = 1 ½ feet.)

Noah was commanded to "bring into the ark two of all living creatures, male and female" (6:19). How did he ever round up and capture all those animals? (6:20; 7:8-9)

What was Noah supposed to gather besides animals? (6:21)

What were the exceptions to the "two of every creature" rule? (7:1-3)

How many people were on the ark? (7:7, 13)

After the ark was loaded, how did Noah get the door closed and sealed? (7:16)

Where did the waters of the flood come from? (7:11-12)

Noah was 600 years old when the flood came (7:6). After he loaded up all the food, animals, and family members, he was on the ark longer than you might expect. Most people know that it rained for 40 days and 40 nights, but that was not the extent of his ark ride. By the time the waters began to recede, the earth was covered for 150 days (7:24). At that time, the ark came to rest on the mountains of Ararat. (Mt. Ararat is 17,000 feet above sea level, though it is thought that the ark landed in that *range* of mountains.) Noah and his family waited in the ark as the waters continued to recede. While the ark was lodged on the mountain,

Noah used birds to gather facts about the state of the earth. How many birds did he send out, and what happened each time? (8:6-12)

On the first day of the first month of Noah's 601st year, the water had dried up from the earth around the ark. It must have been an exciting New Year's party as Noah took off the covering from the ark (8:13). But it took close to two months for the rest of the earth to dry out. Only then did God allow Noah to bring the animals and his family out of the ark.

Noah, his family, and the animals had entered the ark seven days before the flood began (7:7-10). The flood began on the 17th day of the second month of Noah's 600th year (7:11). Noah and crew finally left the ark on the 27th day of the second month of Noah's 601st year (8:14-16). So Noah's stay on the ark was somewhere in the neighborhood of one year and 10 days.

Read Genesis 8:15–9:17 and answer the following questions.

What was the first thing Noah did upon leaving the ark? (8:20)

What was God's response to Noah's action? (8:21-22)

What were God's instructions to Noah's family and the animals before they came out of the ark? (8:16-17)

What command did God add to His instructions *after* Noah came out of the ark? (9:1)

How did man's relationship with animals change after the flood? (9:2-4)

What restrictions did God place on eating meat? Why? (9:4-6)

Why did God institute capital punishment (the death penalty for murder)? (9:5-6)

What was God's covenant (promise) to Noah and his descendants after the flood? (9:11)

After the flood, God promised that a rainbow would be a sign of His covenant with Noah. God didn't flood the earth because He *wanted* to. It was a necessary measure to slow the spread of evil on the earth. It is only because of God's great love that mankind was spared at all. But it didn't take long for sin to pollute the earth again. Read Genesis 9:20-23. What did Noah do after leaving the ark that led to sin?

Even though this is the first mention of wine in the Bible, from

Matthew 24:38 it is apparent that Noah would have known the effects of drinking. How did Noah's drinking binge affect him?

Now read Genesis 9:24-29. How did his drinking affect his family?

Just in case you think Noah was a little severe in his condemnation of Ham and his descendants, you need to know that the Hebrew word translated "saw" in Genesis 9:22 means "gazed with satisfaction." In other words, Ham seemed to think it was pretty funny to see Dad lying naked inside his tent, and thought his brothers might enjoy a laugh as well. But the two older brothers had more respect for their father, and devised a way to cover him without embarrassing him (and themselves).

In the last session you saw that Adam and Eve's sin made them aware of their nakedness. In this case, Ham's reaction to Noah's nakedness made Noah aware that sin was still present on the earth. Ham's descendants had to suffer the consequences of his sin.

STARTING OVER

Genesis 10 lists the descendants of each of Noah's sons and where they settled. You may recognize some of the cities they built, if not the names of the people themselves. Verse 11 records the building of Nineveh, which will be discussed in this series (Book #4) in connection with Jonah. Sodom and Gomorrah are mentioned in verse 19, and these two cities will be important landmarks in the next session. Another city was intended to be built, but never came to completion. Read Genesis 11:1-9 and answer the following questions.

What was unusual about the world at this time?

What was going to be special about the city the people wanted to build?

What kind of attitude did the people seem to have?

Why do you think God was so displeased with the people? (You may want to reread His instructions to Noah in Genesis 9:1.)

How did God take care of the problem?

Genesis 11:10-26 provides the family tree from Shem (Noah's son) to Abram, who will be the main character in the next session.

JOURNEY INWARD

The stories of Noah and the Tower of Babel should cause us to consider the importance of **obedience**—to God and to those in authority over us. For example, what situations do you sometimes face where it seems you are the only godly person in a crowd of unbelievers?

How do you usually handle those situations in which you are the only one who feels the obligation to obey God's instructions for the proper way to live?

Have you ever felt like God wanted you to do something that might seem a little foolish or embarrassing in front of non-Christians? (One example: giving thanks for a meal in a public restaurant.) In such cases are you usually more influenced by God's desires or by the presence of the non-Christians?

The next time you face one of those situations, think of Noah. In a time and country where boating was certainly not the #1 sport, God asked him to build a three-story, 450-foot houseboat and floating zoo. Imagine what the neighbors must have thought (and said)! But then imagine what those same people thought when it began to rain and the water reached their ankles . . . and knees . . . and waists.

The Apostle Paul reminds us that "the foolishness of God is wiser than man's wisdom" (1 Corinthians 1:25). In other words, what seems to be the silliest thing God asks of us is a better idea than the smartest plan we can come up with ourselves—even if His request doesn't seem so great at the time.

Noah didn't mind looking foolish for God, and his faithfulness saved his entire family—not to mention the whole of mankind. If you are willing to risk looking a little foolish for God, do you think your actions could have a positive effect on other people? If so, how?

Perhaps you don't mind too much trying to obey God, but how excited are you about following the instructions of a parent or teacher you don't agree with? Do you think it's important to obey even their "foolish" commands? Why or why not?

List at least three things you might do this week that could show your obedience to God and concern for other people if you weren't so concerned about what your friends might think or say.

▌

Now ask God for the courage to do just one of those things this week. (Start with an easy one. If it doesn't kill you to try that one, follow it up later with some of the other ones on your list.)

 SNAPSHOTS

Noah's Ark:	Because God saw how wicked men had become, he decided to destroy every living creature on earth by sending a flood. But Noah was righteous, so God preserved his life by having him build an ark that would save him and his family from drowning.
Key Verse:	"Never again will I curse the ground because of man, even though every inclination of his heart is evil from childhood. And never again will I destroy all living creatures, as I have done" (Genesis 8:21).
Etc.:	(Your own questions, comments, observations)

A LARGE ORDER OF FAITH—TO GO

(Genesis 12–23)

Imagine you own a luxurious manor in Hawaii and live there with your parents, brothers and sisters, and a large assortment of pets. (Or if this is actually your lifestyle, you won't have to imagine.) You have lots of money, and anything you need or want is available to you. One day you take a break from surfing, lying in the sun, and watching members of the opposite sex stroll by in bathing suits to listen to your favorite song on your state-of-the-art stereo headphones. Suddenly, God's voice comes through your Walkman. He calls you by name and says, "I want you to pack up your stuff, gather your parents, brothers, sisters, and pets, and move."

Naturally, one of your first questions is, "Where to?" But God's answer is, "Don't worry about it. I'll show you when we get there. It's a nice place. Trust Me. Oh, by the way, all of you will have to tent camp for a couple of years until you get there."

Would you move? Or would you stay where you are and enjoy the sure things at your disposal?

JOURNEY ONWARD

A man named Abram once had a similar choice to make. He lived closer to the Euphrates River than the Pacific Ocean, and he was already married. But he *did* come from a well-to-do family and was instructed to leave his homeland to go to an unknown place that God would show him. Abram was originally from a city named Ur, but his father (Terah) had begun a journey to Canaan, arrived at a place called Haran, and settled there instead of moving on. The eleventh chapter of Genesis ends with Terah's death in Haran.

Read Genesis 12:1-7 and answer the following questions.

What promise(s) did God make Abram at Haran?

What did Abram have to do to claim God's promise?

After Abram obeyed God, what promise did God add to the things He had already promised?

A famine in Canaan forced Abram and Sarai to go to Egypt. But just before they got there, Abram realized that his life might be in danger because Sarai was a beautiful woman. He thought that perhaps if the Egyptians discovered that Sarai was his wife, they would kill him so she could be added to one of their harems. So Abram instructed Sarai to say she was his sister (just in case anyone asked).

It turns out that Abram's suspicions were justified. The Egyptians *did* take notice of Sarai's beauty. The officials of the Pharaoh saw her and told their master about her, in case he was interested. He was. In fact, he gave Abram sheep, cattle, donkeys, servants, and camels. It seems that Abram was willing to go along with this charade, even though it meant his beautiful wife would be given to another man.

But God intervened. What did God do to discourage Pharaoh from taking Sarai as his wife, and how did Pharaoh respond? (12:17-20)

As Abram and his family returned from Egypt, they ran into some problems. God had blessed Abram and his nephew, Lot. Both had many possessions—including large flocks and herds, which required much food and water. Since Abram and Lot were traveling together, their herdsmen began to argue with each other because the land would not support all the animals. Abram suggested that they separate, and he gave Lot first choice of where to live. (This was unusual. Abram should have had first choice, since he was older.) Lot chose the fertile land along the plain of the Jordan. And since this was such prime real estate, many other people already lived there in two major cities—Sodom and Gomorrah. Abram was left to live in the land of Canaan, which didn't look so good at first sight, but which was the land God had led him to inherit.

What promise(s) did God make Abram at this point, and how did Abram respond? (13:14-18)

It wasn't too long before Lot began to regret his decision to live in
Sodom. A group of kings decided to make war on the kings of Sodom,
Gomorrah, and three of their allies. In the conflict that followed, Lot
and his family were captured and taken by the enemy army. When a
messenger told Abram what had happened, he gathered together 318
of his men and went to rescue Lot and his family. His men successfully
defeated the enemy army. After the battle Abram was confronted by
two men. Who were they, and how did Abram respond to each one?
(14:18-24)

- Man #1

- Man #2

By this time, God had promised to make Abram "a great nation" (12:2);
to make his descendants as "the dust of the earth" (13:16); and now to
make his descendants as the stars of the heavens (15:5). Try to imagine the stars in the sky—before electricity and skyscrapers, when
Abram could see thousands of stars at night. Why do you think it might
have been difficult for Abram to believe all these things that God had
promised?

At first Abram thought God meant he should "adopt" (so to speak) his
servant, Eliezer of Damascus, and make him an heir—a practice which
was customary for childless couples back then (15:3). But God said that
Abram would father the son that would be his heir (15:4). Though having a child seemed impossible, "Abram believed the Lord, and He credited it to him as righteousness" (15:6). Then God gave Abram a sign of
His power, a prophecy, and a promise. What were they?

- The sign (15:7-11, 17)—

● The prophecy (15:12-15)—

● The promise (15:18)—

"GOD, I'M CONFUSED!"

Even after God tried to make Himself clear, Abram didn't fully compre-
hend God's intentions. Sarai was still childless, so she suggested that
Abram have a baby by her handmaid—another practice that was customary at the time. So Hagar (the handmaid) was "promoted" from
maid to concubine. (A concubine was sort of an "unofficial" wife, yet entitled to many of the legal rights of a wife. Concubines were often used
to bear and raise heirs.)

But what happened after Hagar became pregnant? (16:4-6)

What promise(s) did God make to Hagar? (16:7-15)

How long had it been since God first promised to make Abram "a great
nation"? (12:2-4; 16:16)

Thirteen more years passed between the action of Genesis chapters 16
and 17. Chapter 17 opens with a confirmation of God's promise to give
Abram many descendants. In fact, God changed Abram's name to sym-
bolize the promise. "Abram" meant "exalted father." But God changed
his name to "Abraham," which means "father of a great number."

Besides promising to make Abraham a great nation, what relationship did God promise to have with Abraham's descendants? (17:7)

In order to help Abraham and his descendants stay aware of God's covenant (promise) to them, God instituted circumcision as a sign. (Circumcision in the Old Testament refers to cutting off the foreskin of the male penis—an operation usually done eight days after birth for a Hebrew child.) God also changed Sarai's name at this time. The change seems minor—from *Sarai* ("My princess") to *Sarah* ("Princess"). But perhaps the name change served to emphasize God's promise to Abraham concerning his wife. What was God's promise? (17:15-16)

How did Abraham—our great model for faith—respond to the news concerning his 90-year-old wife? (17:17)

Who was to be the son through whom God would fulfill His covenant with Abraham? (17:19, 21)

What would the future hold for Abraham's other son? (17:19-20)

Genesis 18 begins with another appearance of the Lord to Abraham, but this encounter seems to be a little different from those in the past. When God spoke to Abraham previously (Genesis 15), it was through a vision (v. 1) and a deep sleep (v. 12). Now, however, it seems that God (18:1) and two angels (18:2; 19:1) appear to Abraham in human form. Perhaps Abraham had no idea who they were at first. The treatment he gave them (food, water for their feet, etc.) was typical of the hospitality of that time and culture. What news did the three heavenly messengers have concerning Sarah? (18:9-10)

How did Sarah respond? Why? (18:11-15)

What news did God and the two angels have concerning Sodom and Gomorrah? (18:16-22)

What was Abraham's response? (18:23-33)

How many godly people would it have taken to prevent God from destroying an entire city? (18:32)

DESTRUCTION OF WICKED CITIES

When the two angels reached Sodom, Lot was at the gate. Much of a city's business was conducted at its gate, suggesting that perhaps Lot was a city official. What can you tell about Lot from his treatment of the two visitors? (19:2-3)

Why do you think Lot insisted the visitors stay in his house? (19:3)

Sodom had quite a reputation for being a center for homosexual activity. (Even today, the word *sodomy* refers to sexual relations between members of the same sex, or between people and animals.) The situation in Sodom had gotten so bad that not even 10 righteous people could be found in the entire city. During Lot's stay in Sodom, how strong was the desire for homosexual relationships? (19:4-9)

[NOTE—Lot's attempt to substitute his virgin daughters for the two visitors appears heartless, but was probably prompted by the laws of hospitality which indicated that a host should do whatever he had to do to protect his guests. Or perhaps Lot sensed that the two visitors were not ordinary men.]

After the crowd turned on Lot, how did he escape? (19:10-11)

The angels told Lot that God planned to destroy Sodom because of its wickedness, and warned him to get all his friends and family out of town.

Even though God was acting in Lot's best interest and trying to protect him and his family, how did they react?

• Lot's sons-in-law (19:14)

• Lot, his wife, and his daughters (19:15-16)

What warning was given Lot and his family as they fled Sodom? (19:17)

Lot's wife disregarded the angels' instructions. Why do you think she disobeyed, and what happened to her? (19:24-26)

Since Lot and his family seemed so hesitant to leave Sodom in the first place, why do you think God spared them? (19:27-29)

God chose to deliver Lot in much the same way He delivered Noah (session 2). That is, He removed a handful of righteous people from a large-scale atmosphere of wickedness, and then brought His judgment upon the wicked ones only. But once again, sin followed soon after God's deliverance. What sin occurred in Lot's case? (19:30-38)

[In later sessions you will see that the descendants of Moab (the Moabites) and Ben-ammi (the Ammonites) eventually became enemies of the Israelites.]

If you read through Genesis 20, it will sound like an instant replay of Genesis 12. Once again, Abraham tried to pass Sarah off as his sister— this time to King Abimelech instead of Pharaoh. What was Abraham's reasoning behind his deception? (20:11)

Abraham was telling the truth to some extent. Sarah *was* his half sister (see 20:12). But any half-truth is also half lie. This is the second time that Abraham—a sincere and righteous man—almost allowed an ungodly person to unknowingly commit adultery with Sarah. Both times God made the truth known to the ungodly rulers before they could defile Sarah. After God intervened, how did Abimelech settle up with Abraham? (20:14-16)

What did Abraham do for Abimelech? (20:17-18)

Sometime after Abraham and Sarah returned home, Abraham had his 100th birthday. And later that year he received quite a present—his son, Isaac, whom 90-year-old Sarah gave birth to. God's promise to make Abraham "a great nation" had been made when Abraham was 75 (12:2-4). How do you think you would react if you had to wait 25 years to receive every promise made to you?

God never breaks His promises, but many times we don't give Him time to act. Like Abraham, we wait a certain length of time and then decide to "help God out" or take things in our own hands. In this case, God waited till it seemed impossible for His promise to come true. (Sarah's body had physically gone beyond the point of bearing or nursing children—so she thought.) But God wanted to teach Abraham that when He says He will do something, He *will* do it.

Even though Abraham and Sarah were elated that Isaac had been born to them, not everyone was happy. Isaac's birth renewed the friction between Sarah and Hagar. How was it resolved, and how did God care for Hagar and her son, Ishmael? (21:8-21)

DISPLAY OF FAITH

But when Isaac was a little older, God made an unusual request of Abraham. What was it? (22:1-2)

The journey to Moriah was about 50 miles and took three days, so

Abraham had plenty of time to think about God's instructions. He split the wood for the offering (22:3), but he also told the people he was with that he would return with Isaac (22:5). Why?

What happened then? (22:6-14)

What was the reward for Abraham's unquestioning obedience? (22:15-19)

Genesis 23 records the events after the death of Sarah, who lived to the age of 127. After her death, Abraham bought a field which contained the cave of Machpelah. The cave became the family burial plot.

 JOURNEY INWARD

In the last session, the story of Noah taught us the value of obedience to God; now Abraham's story teaches us of the **opportunity** that God provides for us—if we determine to obey Him.

Why do you think God sometimes asks us to do hard (or even "impossible") things?

Abraham didn't receive many of the things God had planned for him until *after* he took those first steps of faith away from his comfortable home. What are some things you could do for God which don't *promise* rewards, but might become very rewarding if you get involved?

What are some activities that you are occasionally involved in that might be compared to living in Sodom? (These could include intentional sins or even sinful acts you don't actually participate in, but that you put up with because of friends, opportunities, etc.)

Have you ever read a promise of God in the Bible, and then tried to make it come true on your own? What happened?

Is sin widespread in your school? If you went there to find all the righteous people, how many people do you think you would find?

If God asked you to give up your most prized possession, what would it be? Would you be willing to "sacrifice" it if He wanted you to?

Hebrews 13:2 gives us a challenge: "Do not forget to entertain strangers, for by so doing some people have entertained angels without knowing it." If the last stranger you came in contact with was an angel in disguise, what kind of treatment did he receive?

 SNAPSHOTS

God's   God told Abram to leave home and travel to a place that
Promise: God would show him, promising to make a great nation

of Abram. Abram took his family and belongings and went. God changed Abram's and Sarai's names to Abraham and Sarah. At the same time, He reaffirmed His covenant to make of them a great nation, be their God, and give them the land of Canaan. Circumcision was instituted as the sign of the covenant.

Isaac: After years of waiting, Sarah gave birth to Isaac. Unexpectedly, God asked Abraham to offer Isaac as a sacrifice to Him; when Abraham showed he would obey, God stopped him and spared the boy.

Key Verse: "Abram believed the Lord, and He credited it to him as righteousness" (Genesis 15:6).

Etc.:   (Your own questions, comments, observations)

FAMILY FEUDING

(Genesis 24–36)

"Mom likes you better!"
"So what? Dad likes *you* better."
"Give me back my stuff."
"It's not yours anymore. I won it fair and square."
"I'm going to *kill* you!"
"I'm telling Mom you said that."
"Sure, go running to Mom . . . you sissy wimp."
"I may be a wimp, but at least I'm not a hairball!"

Does this sound like a conversation between you and your brothers and
sisters? Or the script of a low-budget TV sitcom? Actually, this ex-
change of thoughts (perhaps not in these exact words) is the gist of an

Old Testament argument between two brothers whom we are going to examine in this session.

You may find it hard to believe, but family relationships recorded in the Bible weren't always smooth ones. Back in the Old Testament, husbands and wives didn't necessarily get along. Parents sometimes favored one child over another. Brothers and sisters competed for their parents' approval. Jealousy and deceit were common. (Nothing like the way things are today, huh?)

They even had a form of blind dates back then. And though you may not be the type to get gushy over romance novels, you've still got to appreciate the love story in Genesis 24. In the last session you studied Abraham—both his unfailing faith in God and his intense love for his son, Isaac. Being the good father that he was, Abraham wanted to make sure Isaac married a godly woman. He knew that the women in Canaan (where Isaac lived) worshiped false gods, so he devised a plan to make sure Isaac could marry a girl who knew the true God.

JOURNEY ONWARD

Read Genesis 24:1-9. What was Abraham's plan to get Isaac a good wife?

Read Genesis 24:10-20. What can you tell about Abraham's servant from this passage (especially vv. 12-14)?

How would Abraham's servant know which woman God had chosen for Isaac?

How long did it take for God to answer Abraham's servant's prayer?

When Abraham's servant was sure that Rebekah was the right woman for Isaac, he gave her gifts of jewelry, invited himself home with her, and didn't forget to stop and thank God (24:22-27). He made arrangements with Rebekah's brother, Laban, to take her back to Canaan, after which he again thanked God and gave Rebekah and her family more gifts. So Abraham's servant made the long journey home accompanied by Rebekah and her maids.

Read Genesis 24:61-67. Was the result of the meeting worth all the trouble? Why?

Even though Isaac and Rebekah's marriage seemed to be a "match made in heaven," it was not without problems. Read Genesis 25:19-21. What was the main problem?

How did Isaac deal with the problem?

When God answered Isaac's request, He did so in a major way. Read Genesis 25:22-26. How was Isaac's prayer answered?

How long had he been waiting to have children? (v. 26)

Even though Jacob and Esau were twins, Esau was the firstborn and entitled to special privileges (including twice the inheritance of any other children). Isaac loved Esau more, because Esau was a hunter and outdoorsman. Rebekah preferred Jacob, who was quiet and liked to hang around the house. Apparently it didn't take too long for a rivalry to develop between the brothers. Read Genesis 25:29-34. What was one early result of the rivalry between Jacob and Esau?

Let the impact of this story sink in. Imagine you've been on a weekend camping trip where the raccoons stole all your food, you couldn't catch a single fish, and all the good roots and berries had already been plucked by an efficient Brownie troop the week before. You return home sunburned, sleepy, and *starved*. And when you get there, your little brother is flipping two extremely large T-bone steaks on the grill. He tells you three things: (1) Mom and Dad aren't home, (2) He has removed all other food from the house, and (3) If you want one of those steaks, you have to promise to give him the car you've been promised for graduation. After the weekend you've had, your mind isn't as clear as it should be, so you figure a car won't do you a whole lot of good after you've starved to death. You agree to your brother's devious deal. But you think, *It's a long time till I graduate. I'll think of some way out of this bargain before I have to turn over my car to that little wimp.* (Keep these thoughts in mind as you continue this session.)

The story of Jacob and Esau is put on hold temporarily as Genesis 26 shifts the emphasis back to Isaac. If you read Genesis 26:1-11, the phrase "Like father, like son" is likely to come to mind. A famine caused Isaac and Rebekah to leave home and travel in a foreign land. (Abraham had gone to Egypt, but Isaac went to the land of the Philistines.) There Isaac feared for his life because Rebekah was so beautiful, so he told everyone she was his sister. The king of the Philistines discovered the truth, and scolded Isaac for his deceit. Then he decreed that no one should harm Isaac or his wife.

While Isaac was in the land of the Philistines, God caused him to be prosperous. The Philistines were jealous, and finally asked him to move away. But it didn't take long for them to come after him and ask for a treaty, to which Isaac agreed. God also renewed with Isaac the covenant He had made previously with Abraham—possession of the land of Canaan, numerous descendants, and other blessings (see 26:2-5, 24).

We also learn that Esau took a couple of wives—both of them Hittite people from the land of Canaan. Isaac and Rebekah were not pleased with his choice of wives. (See 26:34-35.) This fact will be important later in this session. Genesis 27 picks up the story of Jacob and Esau again.

STOLEN BLESSING

This familiar story reads like a spy novel or an episode of "Mission: Impossible." Isaac had become blind in his old age. One day he called Esau to him and asked him to go hunt some meat and prepare a special meal for him to eat before he died. After Esau brought him the meal, Isaac was to give him his blessing. (Isaac's expectation of death was a little premature. He lived several years after this incident.)

Isaac didn't know it, but Rebekah was eavesdropping on his conversation. She came up with a plan for Jacob to outsmart Esau. What was it? (27:5-17)

The plan almost didn't work. Isaac had a couple of suspicions. Read Genesis 27:18-29. What caused Isaac to doubt what Jacob was saying? (Note verses 20 and 22.)

Isaac couldn't see, and his hearing caused him to doubt the truthfulness of Jacob's presentation. But his other three senses persuaded him to give his blessing to Jacob. How did Jacob convince his father through:

- Touch?

- Taste?

- Smell?

Now read Genesis 27:30-40. As soon as Jacob left with Isaac's blessing, Esau entered the room expecting to receive it. How did Isaac respond to the news that he had been deceived?

How did Esau respond, and how did he plan to get even with Jacob? (27:41)

Naturally, Rebekah was alarmed when she heard that her favorite son was in danger. Again, she was quick to come up with a plan for Jacob's well-being. What was her plan? (27:42–28:5)

One night on the way to Haran, Jacob had a strange dream. In the space below, illustrate (either verbally or artistically) what he dreamed (28:10-15).

Jacob's dream was significant. It verified that God was going to give Jacob what he had tried so hard to gain all along. Jacob had used high-pressure tactics and trickery to get Esau's birthright; but in the dream, God reveals that Jacob was the one whom He intended to receive the blessings of his fathers in the first place. The original promise made to Abraham, and then Isaac, was now made to Jacob. How did Jacob react to the dream? (28:16-17)

How did he respond to the news God had given him? (28:18-22)

RACHEL AND LEAH
Jacob continued his journey to Haran. When he got there, he asked a group of shepherds for directions to Laban's house. At that exact

moment, Laban's daughter Rachel approached them with her sheep, and the shepherds told Jacob who she was. Jacob told her who he was, and she ran off to get Laban. After Jacob had stayed a month, he and Laban made an agreement concerning Jacob's work. What was the deal they made, what went wrong with the deal, and how was the deal resolved? (29:14-30)

After all the tricks Jacob had pulled on other people—such as conning Esau out of his birthright and deceiving his father for the blessing—Jacob finally learned what it was like to be on the receiving end of someone's deceit. And just as Jacob and Esau had a continual battle going against each other, now Rachel and Leah begin to compete for Jacob's attention.

Read Genesis 29:31–30:24. As you do, fill in the following chart with the names of the women who bore children for Jacob, and put the names of the children underneath each mother.

MOTHER #1   MOTHER #2   MOTHER #3   MOTHER #4
_____   _____   _____   _____

After Rachel finally had a son, Jacob desired to return to his homeland. Laban wanted him to stay, and Jacob agreed to remain for a while. He made a deal to split the herds with Laban, so they could tell which animals were Laban's and which were Jacob's. Soon Jacob became very prosperous, which made Laban and his sons jealous. Actually, in spite of everything Jacob was trying to do on his own, it was God who made Jacob prosper (31:6-9).

At this point God told Jacob it was time to return to Canaan. Jacob called for Leah and Rachel (who stole her father's household idols to take with her), and they left without telling Laban. When Laban discovered they had gone, he followed and caught up with them 10 days later. He was angry at their leaving without telling him, but he seemed angriest that his idols were missing. Jacob, not knowing that Rachel had taken them, told Laban that if he could find them, the person who had them would be put to death. How did Rachel avoid being discovered? (31:33-35)

Jacob and Laban then discussed their grievances with each other and finally made a covenant of peace. The next day Laban gave his daughters and grandchildren his blessing and a kiss, and returned home.

As soon as Jacob was rid of one adversary (Laban), he had to begin to worry about another one (Esau, who had threatened his life 20 years earlier). But God gave Jacob a sign that He was still with him. What was the sign? (32:1-2)

Jacob sent messengers ahead of him who came back and reported that Esau was on the way to meet him with 400 men. Jacob became a little worried, but of course it didn't take him long to come up with a plan.

How did he prepare to confront Esau? (32:7-21)

Jacob spent that night alone, and it was a most unusual night. Read Genesis 32:23-31 and answer the following questions.

- What did Jacob do all night?

- Who do you think his opponent was?

- The name *Israel* means "he struggles with God." Why do you think Jacob was given that name?

After 20 years of running away and hiding from Esau, the moment of truth finally came as the brothers met again. Read Genesis 33:1-15 and describe their reunion.

Jacob and his family hadn't been in Canaan long before they faced more trouble. Usually you hear about the sons of Jacob (or Israel), but this time the daughter of Jacob was involved. What happened to Dinah? (34:1-4)

In what emotional state were Dinah's brothers when they heard what had happened? (34:7)

Even though Shechem really loved Dinah, his family saw the potential benefits of becoming Jacob's "in-laws." What was their motive? (34:23)

What was their plan? (34:9-10)

What condition did Jacob's sons give Shechem's family before agreeing to their proposition? (34:13-17)

What happened before the marriage took place? (34:24-31)

Genesis 35 returns to the relationship between God and Jacob. God told Jacob to return to Bethel (where Jacob had dreamed of the ladder of angels) and build an altar. So Jacob gathered his household and prepared to leave, but what did he do first? (35:2-5)

After Jacob reached Bethel and built his altar, God confirmed the same promises He had made previously to Abraham and Isaac—to make a nation of him and give land to his descendants (35:11-13). Then as Jacob's family moved on from Bethel, Rachel gave birth to another son. But complications set in and she died giving birth. What was Rachel's other son's name? (35:16-18)

Not long afterward, Jacob's father, Isaac, died too. The descendants of Jacob and Esau are listed in Genesis 35:23–36:43.

JOURNEY INWARD

While the events of this chapter are fresh in your mind, think about your own **family relationships.** What lessons can you learn from Jacob about deceiving others?

Do you think Jacob could blame his tendency to deceive others on his family upbringing? Or do you think he was more at fault? Defend your answer.

Are you more like Jacob or Esau? Explain.

What characteristics do you see in your parent(s) that you want to imitate?

What characteristics do you see in your parent(s) that you want to avoid?

How long does it take you to make up after you have had a fight with a family member? What would it take for you to reduce that length of time in future arguments?

List all the unresolved problems you can think of in your family.

In the weeks to come, challenge yourself to reduce the size of the above list. First select all the situations which are at least partly *your* fault. In those cases, *you* can do something to resolve them. Ask (or grant) forgiveness for any wrongdoing. Or if you have destroyed someone's property, make arrangements to replace it. Start with whatever *you* can do. In the other instances, you can follow Isaac's example when Rebekah couldn't give him a child. He prayed and God answered. Through prayer, leave the other unresolved problems on your list in God's hands. (And don't be surprised if He takes care of the items you leave to Him before you settle the ones *you're* working on.)

 SNAPSHOTS

Rebekah, Esau, and Jacob:	Isaac married Rebekah, and they became the parents of twins, Jacob and Esau. Esau was a hunter, and Jacob liked to stay at home. Though Esau was the firstborn, Jacob maneuvered him into selling his birthright.
Jacob's Dream:	Because Esau wanted to kill him, Jacob fled to his Uncle Laban in Haran. On the way, he dreamed of a stairway or ladder to heaven, and the Lord telling him that he and his descendants would be given the land where he was.
Key Verse:	"May the Lord keep watch between you and me when we are away from each other" (Genesis 31:49).
Etc.:	(Your own questions, comments, observations)

BROTHERS AND OTHER BOTHERS

(Genesis 37–50)

You've probably heard of comedian Rodney Dangerfield. He made a name (and a fortune) for himself by telling jokes about how he never gets any respect. Rodney is better than most people about getting a re-action from others, but *everybody* seems to want to exaggerate their pressures and problems in order to get attention for their "suffering."

"You think *your* parents are bad? *My* parents grounded me for six months because I got home two minutes late after taking my girlfriend home from prayer meeting." [Translation: Prayer meeting was over at 7 P.M. You were grounded for two weeks because you got home at 11:30 P.M. (instead of 10 P.M. when you were supposed to), and you had lipstick all over your face and shirt collar.]

"Boy, it's a good thing you missed football practice today. Coach Neanderthal worked us for three hours in the blazing 100-degree heat. I was up against Ironhead 'Killer' Bronski. He almost ripped my arm off. I'd show you the bruises, but they're just too gruesome." [Translation: You managed to break a sweat in the 85-degree weather. Oh, yeah. You also got a boo-boo on your arm.]

Something inside us makes us want to make our pressures sound worse than anyone else's. But this session brings you the account of a guy who had every right to complain about the pressures he faced. In fact, his truthful life story could probably top our best exaggerations. Yet he doesn't whine a bit about his circumstances or try to get sympathy from other people.

JOURNEY ONWARD

In the last session we saw that Jacob (Israel) fathered 12 sons through 4 different women. What pressures do you think you might face if you lived in a family with 11 brothers, a sister, a father, and 4 mothers?

Read Genesis 37:1-4. Why do you think Jacob liked Joseph best?

Why do you think Joseph's brothers didn't like him?

Read Genesis 37:5-11. What do you think Joseph's dreams meant?

How did Joseph's family members respond when Joseph told them his dreams?

∎

Read Genesis 37:12-36. What happened when Jacob sent Joseph to check on his brothers?

∎

How did Jacob respond when he was told that Joseph had been killed?

∎

What eventually happened to Joseph?

∎

Genesis 38 interrupts the story of Joseph (sort of a "Meanwhile, back at the ranch . . . " chapter), so it is often overlooked. But this chapter contains several things that should be noted—such as excessive sin, responsibility, and hypocrisy, to name a few.

Judah (one of Jacob's 12 sons) married a woman from another town, and they had three sons. The oldest son, Er, grew up and married a girl named Tamar. What is Er remembered for? (38:7)

∎

After Er's death, the custom of the time dictated that the next oldest son (Onan, in this case) should marry the widow of his brother. The reason for this custom (which later became a law) was to provide children to care for the widow and continue the family line of the person who had died. Onan probably realized that Judah's inheritance might go to the son of the firstborn instead of the second born. So Onan (the second born) slept with Tamar, but didn't complete the sexual act. It is likely that Onan didn't want to father a child who could receive the inheritance he thought should be his own (38:9).

What was the result of Onan's selfish act? (38:8-10)

▌

After Judah lost his two oldest sons, Er and Onan, he didn't want to take any chances with his last one, Shelah. It should have been Shelah's responsibility to give Tamar a child, but Judah postponed the marriage with the excuse that he wanted to give Shelah time to "grow up" (v. 11). As time passed and Tamar saw that her marriage to Shelah wasn't likely to take place, she decided to act on her own. She went to a location where she knew Judah would be, and disguised herself as a prostitute. Judah, not realizing she was his daughter-in-law, made a bargain to sleep with her. He offered as payment a young animal from his flock. She asked for a "deposit" until he gave her the animal, so Judah gave her his seal and staff. After she slept with Judah, Tamar took Judah's things home with her. When Judah sent his servant with a young goat to regain his possessions, he was told that no prostitute had been there.

Tamar became pregnant from her encounter with Judah, and when he found out about it (not having any idea that he was the father), he threw a fit. He was planning to have Tamar put to death because, after all, how dare a relative of his commit adultery! But as she was being "arrested," Tamar showed Judah his own seal and staff and said something like, "You might want to kill the guy too. Here are some clues to help you find him."

Judah suddenly realized what must have happened. He also realized how Tamar must have felt when he refused to let her marry Shelah. He allowed her to live (what else could he do?), and her pregnancy resulted in twin boys. What was unusual about their birth? (38:27-30)

▌

It may seem to make little difference which of those twins was actually the firstborn. But the noteworthy fact about the birth of Perez is that it is through him that the line of Judah is traced to David, and eventually to Jesus (Matthew 1:1-16, esp. v. 3).

Now, back to the story of Joseph. Even as an Egyptian slave, God made Joseph prosper. Soon he was placed in charge of Potiphar's entire household. And in addition to being successful, Joseph was a hunk as far as the ladies were concerned (39:6). That combination of qualities was too much for Mrs. Potiphar to resist, and she began to try to seduce Joseph "day after day" (39:10). But Joseph always refused. Why? (39:8-9)

Then one day Joseph was alone in the house with Mrs. P. and got close enough for her to make a grab at him. She hung on to Joseph's robe while he escaped, but what did she tell Potiphar when he got home? (39:13-20)

What did Potiphar do?

God continued to bless everything Joseph did, even in prison. Joseph was put in charge of everyone in the jail, and made friends with a couple of Pharaoh's servants who had offended the king. Read Genesis 40. Why were the cupbearer and the baker sad—besides being in jail, that is?

Describe the cupbearer's dream and Joseph's interpretation.

Describe the baker's dream and Joseph's interpretation.

How was Joseph rewarded for successfully interpreting their dreams?

Two years later Joseph was still in jail—until Pharaoh had a couple of dreams of his own. What were Pharaoh's two dreams? (41:1-7)

Pharaoh sent for Joseph, who was quick to give God all the credit for his ability to interpret dreams (41:14-16). He gave Pharaoh God's message—a seven-year period of abundance, followed by a severe seven-year famine, was on the way. What advice did Joseph give Pharaoh, and how did Pharaoh respond to Joseph's suggestions? (41:33-37)

How did Joseph's life change as a result? (41:38-45)

Put yourself in Joseph's place at this point. You're 30 years old. The last time you saw your home and parents was shortly after your 17th birthday. Since then you've been sold into slavery by your own brothers, threatened with death, falsely accused of attempted rape, thrown into jail, and forgotten by the friends you made along the way. Suddenly you are given a position that makes you number two person in one of the most powerful nations in the world. With your position you get expensive jewelry, fancy clothes, your own "wheels" (a chariot), and

BROTHERS AND OTHER BOTHERS **63**

even a spouse. (You haven't even had a date in 13 years, and then BOOM, you're married!)

Joseph's marriage resulted in a couple of sons. He named his older son Manasseh and his other son Ephraim. They were both born during the seven years of abundance in Egypt. Then the famine hit hard, just as Joseph had predicted. And since Joseph had proven that his God knew what He was doing, Pharaoh let Joseph run the whole show (41:55). The famine wasn't limited to Egypt—it also hit Canaan, where Joseph's family still lived.

GUESS WHO'S COMING TO EGYPT?

The action in Genesis 42 shifts back to Joseph's father and brothers. When they began to run out of food, Jacob sent his 10 oldest sons to Egypt to get grain. It appears that Benjamin, the youngest son, had replaced Joseph as Jacob's favorite. (Joseph and Benjamin were the only two sons of Rachel.) So Benjamin stayed at home (42:4).

When the 10 brothers got to Egypt, they had to deal with the man in charge—that's right, Joseph. He recognized his brothers right away, but they didn't recognize him. After all, he was probably dressed as Egyptian royalty, wore an Egyptian hairstyle, and spoke with an Egyptian accent. (Since Joseph was 30 when he left prison and 7 abundant years had passed since *then,* he was at least 37. His brothers hadn't seen him in 20 years.) What story did Joseph's brothers give him? (42:13)

▌

Joseph may have become a little alarmed to see that his younger brother was not with the rest of the group, and he accused his brothers of being spies. He said they could only prove that they weren't spies by bringing back their younger brother. And to make sure they returned, he insisted on keeping one of the older brothers imprisoned in Egypt. Which brother stayed? (42:24)

▌

How did Joseph's brothers explain all the "bad luck" that was happening to them? (42:21-23)

What unusual instructions did Joseph give his servants (concerning his brothers)? (42:25-26)

What effect did those instructions have on his brothers? (42:27-28)

When the nine brothers got home, they told Jacob everything that had happened. While they were still blaming everything that went wrong on their harsh treatment of Joseph 20-plus years ago, they hadn't yet told Jacob the truth. He still thought Joseph was dead (42:36).

Jacob was in no hurry to send Benjamin off to Egypt. It seems he would have been willing to lose Simeon if he could have insured Benjamin's safety. But why did he finally change his mind and allow Benjamin to be taken to Egypt? (43:1-14)

Since no one knew what to expect when they got back to Egypt, the 10 brothers (including Benjamin, not including Simeon) loaded up with gifts and twice the money the 9 brothers had found in their sacks before. But when they arrived in Egypt, Joseph told them that he had the money they had given him before. He suggested that God must have put more money in their sacks. Then Joseph brought out Simeon and had his servants prepare a meal for the 11 brothers. When the 11 brothers got ready to leave Egypt this time, Joseph gave his servants instructions similar to those he had given before. But what variation did he make in his instructions this time? (44:1-2)

The 11 brothers hadn't gotten far when Joseph's men stopped them and accused them of stealing a special silver cup. Joseph's servants found it in Benjamin's sack. (After all, that's where they had put it.) Then they took everyone back to "stand trial" before Joseph. How did Joseph suggest they settle the matter, and why do you think Joseph made the suggestion? (44:14-17)

Genesis 44:18-34 describes Judah's defense before Joseph. Basically, he said that Jacob wouldn't be able to handle the loss of Benjamin. How did Judah suggest that they resolve the problem? (44:33-34)

Joseph had given his brothers every opportunity to "sell out" Benjamin. But after he noted their sincerity and changed attitudes, he could keep his secret no longer. He sent away all the Egyptians and told his brothers who he was. The trauma of the moment was almost too much for him. "He wept so loudly that the Egyptians heard him, and Pharaoh's household heard about it" (45:2). Joseph's sudden "transformation" caused his brothers to become "terrified" and speechless. Why do you think they were so scared?

What was the first question Joseph asked them? (45:3)

Read Genesis 45:4-8 and summarize Joseph's attitude toward his brothers and toward all that had happened to him in Egypt.

With five years of famine left to come, Joseph instructed his brothers to pick up Jacob and bring him to Egypt where there was plenty of food.

But before he sent them away, they all had a good cry (45:14-15). How did Jacob respond to the news that his "dead" son Joseph was "ruler of all Egypt"? (45:26-28)

On the way to Egypt, God appeared to Jacob in a vision at night (much the way He had appeared to him previously). God wanted to assure Jacob that it was His will that Jacob go to Egypt, and that God would return His people to the Promised Land eventually (46:1-4). How many people moved from Canaan to Egypt? (46:26-27)

Pharaoh made sure Joseph's family settled in the best part of Egypt, an area called Goshen. After 17 years in Egypt, Jacob realized that he was close to death. He made Joseph promise not to bury him in Egypt, and then called his sons together to bless them. Notice in Genesis 48:5-6 that Jacob gave Joseph's sons (Manasseh and Ephraim) equal treatment with his own sons. (Later you will see that the 12 tribes of Israel will include Manasseh and Ephraim as well as Jacob's own sons.)

When it came time for Jacob to bless Joseph's sons, he crossed his hands so that his right hand was on Ephraim (the younger son). And even though Joseph objected, Jacob explained that God was once again going to favor the younger son (48:13-20).

Genesis 49 contains Jacob's blessings for his sons. After Jacob's blessings, he died. Joseph, true to his oath, returned him to the cave of Machpelah (in Canaan) after having him embalmed (49:28–50:14). Joseph was saddened at his father's death, but his older brothers had a different reaction. What did they think after Jacob died? (50:15-18)

Were their fears justified? (50:19-21)

Joseph lived to be 110 years old. Before he died, he gave some specific (and somewhat unusual) instructions. What was his last request? (50:24-25)

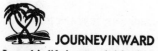 **JOURNEY INWARD**

Joseph's life is a model for how we should handle **pressures**. In each of the categories below, make a list of the pressures you face in that category and then think of some steps you can take to resolve them.

PRESSURES	STEPS TOWARD HANDLING YOUR PRESSURES

HOME

SCHOOL

DATING

OTHER

NOTE: If any of your pressures seem unbearable, remember that God remained aware of and in control of Joseph's situation at all times. Sure, Joseph had to go through a lot of inconvenience, but God eventually made it all worthwhile—both for Joseph and his entire family, and for the people whose lives were saved during the famine. (Often the first move you need to make is to actually take the steps you've listed.)

The next session moves into the Book of Exodus. So far in our study of Genesis, we have seen the growth of sin, the wickedness of the world in general, and the often tragic effects of one person's sin on someone else. Cain's jealousy killed Abel. Noah's drunkenness prompted a sinful response from Ham. Lot's decision to live in Sodom eventually resulted in the deaths of some of his daughters, his wife's reluctance to leave, and the sexually immoral acts of his other daughters. Abraham's misrepresentation of Sarah brought plagues on Pharaoh's and Abimelech's houses. In the last session we saw how the widespread practice of lies and deceit in Isaac's home caused problems for almost everyone. Now, in this session, we saw a guy named Er who was *so* bad that God didn't think he should live any longer. It's hard to imagine how much wickedness it would take for God to personally step in and strike someone down, but in this rare instance He did.

We need to let go of the sins we secretly enjoy—and we all have them. We hold grudges. We cheat on tests. We go a little further than we know we should on dates. If we don't begin to deal with the little sins in our lives, sin becomes a lifestyle and causes problems that prevent us from receiving all the good things God wants to give us. Take a few minutes to list the "little" sins in your life.

As you review your list of "little" sins, determine not to let them control your life. One lesson you should have learned from the life of Joseph is the power of *preparation*. When Joseph had the opportunity to have sex with Mrs. Potiphar, he was prepared with an answer why he shouldn't. When the seven years of famine hit, Joseph was ready for those hard times because he had maintained a relationship with God through the good times and was prepared for the worst.

As corny as it might sound, youth is a time to prepare for the future—to iron out the wrinkles of doubt and inconsistency in your life. Close this session with prayer that God will help you in those "pressurized" areas where you *say* you want to follow God's will for your life, but *act* otherwise.

 SNAPSHOTS

Joseph: Joseph, one of Jacob's sons by Rachel, was Jacob's favorite son and the least favorite brother of the others. His brothers sold him into slavery, telling their father he was dead. Joseph ended up a servant in the house of Potiphar, whose wife tried to seduce Joseph; but he refused. She accused him of rape and he landed in jail. There he interpreted the dreams of a cupbearer and baker.

Pharaoh: Later, Joseph interpreted Pharaoh's dreams about famine. Pharaoh put Joseph in charge of storing food and made him second ruler over Egypt.

Family: The famine drove Joseph's brothers to Egypt to find food. After testing their sincerity to see whether they had changed, Joseph was reunited with his family and brought them to Egypt to live.

Key Verse: "The Lord was with Joseph and gave him success in whatever he did" (Genesis 39:23).

Etc.:   (Your own questions, comments, observations)

HERO MOE VS. NO-NO PHARAOH: PEOPLE GO

(Exodus 1–12)

A few years ago the *Star Wars* movie trilogy made a tremendous impact on the youth of the world. *Star Wars* creatures of all shapes and colors were everywhere—bubble gum cards, dolls, cartoons, etc. The success of the movies was partially due to the tremendous special effects, exotic settings in space, and dynamic acting. But the underlying popularity of the movies had to do with their successful portrayal of a tense battle between the forces of evil (represented by Darth Vader) and the forces of good (represented by the youthful and naive Luke Skywalker). Millions of people crowded into theaters to see if the reluctant hero could possibly outwit and overpower his wicked nemesis.

George Lucas, the creator and director, might disagree, but the plot of

Star Wars was nothing new. In fact, it is basically the same story we will see in this session covering the first few chapters of Exodus. (And this story *is* true!)

 JOURNEY ONWARD

The Hebrew people living in Egypt had prospered under the leadership of Joseph and under the Egyptian leaders who succeeded him after his death. But suddenly a king was appointed who knew nothing of Joseph. He saw the great numbers of Hebrew people and became aware that they had the potential to form alliances with Egypt's enemies and defeat the Egyptians.

What was Pharaoh's plan to prevent the Israelites from becoming too numerous? (Exodus 1:8-14)

When Pharaoh's first plan didn't work, what did he try? (1:15-21)

Plan B didn't work either, so then what did Pharaoh command? (1:22)

Exodus 2:1-10 contains the familiar story of Moses' birth. His mother hid him, but when he got too old to be kept hidden, she placed him in a waterproof basket and set him in the Nile River. Moses was discovered by the daughter of Pharaoh, and when she found him he was crying. She felt sorry for him and decided to adopt him (another example of God's perfect timing).

What arrangements did the princess make for nursing and rearing the baby? (2:7-10)

▮

About 40 years elapse between Exodus 2:10 and 2:11 (Acts 7:23). No doubt Moses was being brought up as a child of the royal household of Egypt, but apparently his loyalty to his Hebrew "roots" was strong. Read Exodus 2:11-15 and answer the following questions:

● During the fight, what decision did Moses have to make?

● What were the results of his decision?

● After Moses made his decision, do you think the Egyptians could ever trust him again?

● Do you think the Israelites trusted him at that point?

Read Exodus 2:16-22. After Moses fled from Egypt, he arrived in Midian (toward the southern part of the Sinai Peninsula). Just prior to his hasty departure, he had seen Hebrews fighting Egyptians and Hebrews fighting other Hebrews. Then as soon as he arrived he found seven young women (the daughters of the priest of Midian) trying to fight off some rude shepherds. Moses chased away the offensive shepherds and helped the women water their father's flocks. But after all his hard work, no one even invited him home to dinner.

The father of the seven girls was named Reuel (2:18) but he also went by another name for which he is better known—Jethro (3:1). He noticed his daughters' early return, asked what had happened, and learned that an "Egyptian" stranger had helped them out. Jethro scolded them for not bringing the guy home, and sent them right back out to get Moses. What was the eventual result of Moses' visit?

Read Exodus 2:23-25 and notice two things. First, God is aware of His people's sufferings, and He is not willing to let them continue indefinitely. Second, note that the Israelites are complaining about their slavery and begging God to do something about it. That fact will be important to remember in future sessions.

Exodus 3:1-10 contains another familiar story. Moses was shepherding Jethro's flocks around Mount Horeb (probably another name for Mount Sinai), when he noticed a bush that was "burning" but wasn't being burned up. Moses thought, *Hmmm. You sure don't see a sight like that very often. Maybe I'll take a closer look.* Why did the bush seem to burn?

What was the good news God had for Moses? (3:7-8)

What was the bad news? (3:9-10)

At this point in his life, Moses was no Charlton Heston. In fact, he gave God a whole list of excuses explaining why he couldn't possibly go to Egypt and lead the Israelites out from under the bondage of Pharaoh. List each of Moses' excuses and God's responses on the following chart.

EXCUSE #1 (3:11)	GOD'S RESPONSE #1 (3:12)
EXCUSE #2 (3:13)	GOD'S RESPONSE #2 (3:14-15)
EXCUSE #3 (4:1)	GOD'S RESPONSE #3 (4:2-9)
EXCUSE #4 (4:10)	GOD'S RESPONSE #4 (4:11-12)
EXCUSE #5 (4:13)	GOD'S RESPONSE #5 (4:14-17)

When Moses finally ran out of excuses, God told him the Egyptians who wanted him dead were now dead themselves, so Moses asked Jethro for permission to return to Egypt. He took the staff of God, his wife (Zipporah), and his two sons (Gershom and Eliezer) with him. But for some reason Moses had not circumcised one of his sons, as God had commanded (Genesis 17:10). Consequently, "the Lord met Moses and was about to kill him" (Exodus 4:24). That's about all we know about the situation, but it was enough to cause Zipporah to circumcise her son immediately (4:25).

At some point, Moses' family returned to Jethro (18:2-4). Perhaps the conflict between Moses and Zipporah on the way to Egypt caused her to "go home to Daddy." We *do* know that at this time God sent Aaron to join Moses. Together the two brothers went to the Israelites, who rejoiced to know that God was concerned about their persecution by the Egyptians (4:29-31).

But Pharaoh wasn't quite so excited. What kind of reaction from Pharaoh had God told Moses to expect? (4:21-23)

How did Pharaoh actually respond to Moses' request to leave? (5:1-2)

Moses and Aaron asked to go on a three days' journey into the wilderness on sort of a "retreat" to worship God. But Pharaoh accused them of only wanting to get the Israelites out of working for a few days. By this time there were hundreds of thousands—possibly millions—of God's people who were enslaved in Egypt. Pharaoh knew that if they all stopped working, not much would be accomplished in his nation. So to make sure everyone knew who was boss, Pharaoh decided to make the Israelites' work more of a challenge. What did he do? (5:6-19)

Did the Israelites appreciate Moses' efforts to get them released? (5:20-21)

Did Moses allow this little setback to increase his faith? What were his thoughts? (5:22-23)

God told Moses everything would be OK and reminded Moses of His unfulfilled promise to Abraham—to give the land of Canaan to His people. The Lord reassured Moses that He was definitely going to deliver the Israelites from Egypt's bondage. So Moses took the good news back to the people of Israel. What was their reaction this time? Why? (6:9)

Even though God expected Moses to go through some challenging experiences, He didn't want him to be unprepared. God knew Pharaoh would ask him for a sign, and He told Moses exactly what to do when Pharaoh challenged him. So when Moses and Aaron stood before Pharaoh the next time, Aaron threw down his staff and it became a serpent. But Pharaoh's magicians somehow simulated the miracle. (Some people think the Egyptians used black magic; some think they used sleight of hand; others think they used snakes that could be "charmed" into a rigid position. The Bible only refers to their abilities as "secret arts" [7:11, 22].) But how was God's power evident to the Egyptians in this situation? (7:11-12)

After Pharaoh refused to be impressed by the power of God, the Lord began to send a series of plagues on Egypt. Notice that God sent the plagues only after first asking Pharaoh nicely (5:1-2) and then again using a sign of His power (7:10).

The account of the plagues is given in Exodus 7:14–12:30. Skim through those chapters and complete the chart on page 77.

What do you think? Was God cruel to send so many plagues on the Egyptians? Defend your answer.

The account of the plagues, though tragic, is comic in spots. For instance, Pharaoh's magicians were so anxious to imitate God's power that they brought forth *more* bloody water and *extra* frogs. (They may

	TYPE OF PLAGUE	CONSE-QUENCES	PHARAOH'S RESPONSE
PLAGUE #1 (7:14-24)			
PLAGUE #2 (7:25–8:15)			
PLAGUE #3 (8:16-19)			
PLAGUE #4 (8:20-32)			
PLAGUE #5 (9:1-7)			
PLAGUE #6 (9:8-12)			
PLAGUE #7 (9:13-35)			
PLAGUE #8 (10:1-20)			
PLAGUE #9 (10:21-29)			
PLAGUE #10 (11; 12:29-32)			

have been good magicians, but perhaps not the brightest people along the Nile.) If they were so great, why didn't they purify the water or remove the frogs? Instead, they only helped God accomplish His plagues against Egypt. And in a later comic incident, the magicians couldn't even stand before Moses and Pharaoh because of their boils (9:11).

God's plagues take on new meaning as we understand the religion of Egypt at that time. Frogs were sacred symbols of fertility, but God made them so fertile that the people couldn't stand the sight (or smell) of them. The sun god, Ra, was also supposed to be popular, but he lost a lot of popularity points while the Egyptians were kept "in the dark" during the ninth plague.

On the tragic side, it's a shame that one man's stubbornness brought about so much grief for so many families. But the Egyptians were given the opportunity to defy Pharaoh, obey God, and avoid some of the plagues (see 9:20), so we can't feel too sorry for those who didn't follow God's instructions.

By this time, many of the Egyptians were wisely beginning to make friends with the Israelites. Moses may not have been respected by Pharaoh, but he was admired by Pharaoh's servants and the Egyptian people. When the Israelites asked for gold and silver articles from their Egyptian neighbors, the Egyptians willingly handed them over. (God had previously told Moses that this would happen [3:21-22].) In fact, the Lord assured Moses that when the Israelites left Egypt, "not a dog will bark" (Exodus 11:7). What do you think He meant?

God wanted to make sure the Israelites remembered their escape from Egypt, so the first thing He did was change their calendar. The month of their departure from Egypt became the first month of their year. And the tenth day of that month was to begin the week of an annual national holiday, the Passover. Read Exodus 12:1-20 and list the things the Israelites were to do during their Passover observance.

Why was this observance to be called Passover? (12:13)

What were the restrictions placed on who could be included in the Passover celebration? (12:43-51)

When God was finally compelled (because of Pharaoh's stubbornness) to send the tenth plague, "there was loud wailing in Egypt, for there was not a house without someone dead" (12:30). Perhaps Pharaoh had chalked up the first nine plagues to magic, but he couldn't this time. After all, *he* had lost his oldest child, and he just wanted Moses and the Israelites to get out of the land and not cause any more trouble.

How many Israelite *men* left Egypt? (12:37)

If you begin with that many men and add a proportionate number of women and children, the total number of *people* leaving Egypt was quite large. In addition to the Israelites, there were also members of other local tribes and a few groups of Egyptians who went along. Add to that mass of people "large droves of livestock" (12:38), and imagine what the scene must have looked like.

How long had the Israelites been in Egypt? (12:40)

Review Genesis 15:13-14. What had God predicted to Abraham?

JOURNEY INWARD

An important element to grasp from this session and apply to your own life is the fact of **God's sovereignty.** In spite of the many bad things that were happening, *God was always in control.*

The Bible tells us, "Everyone must submit himself to the governing authorities, for there is no authority except that which God has established" (Romans 13:1). With this in mind, do you think Moses' parents were wrong to disobey Pharaoh's orders to save their son? Why?

Is it ever right to disobey laws? If so, when?

Do you think Moses was justified in killing the Egyptian that was beating the Hebrew? Or do you think that he had other options? Explain.

Sometimes we try to justify our sins by finding a good enough reason and expecting God to understand. But sin is sin. What are some recent actions you have tried to justify, even though you knew they weren't quite right?

Moses must have thought he had hit rock bottom when he suddenly went from being a ruler in Egypt to being a shepherd in Midian. Yet it was during his desert experience that God revealed Himself to Moses, and that's when Moses rapidly matured. Can you think of any instances in your past when you were humbled, but learned a good spiritual lesson in the process?

God often uses people to accomplish what He wants done. He doesn't operate that way for *His* benefit—He does it for *our* benefit. Because he let God use him, Moses benefited from the experience. But Moses' excuses almost kept him from becoming a better and stronger person. What are some of the excuses you use to get out of doing things you think God might want you to do?

As you struggle with your excuses and perceived shortcomings, try to keep in mind what Moses learned: *God is in control—no matter what.* You can trust a sovereign God with all your weaknesses and know that you will succeed on His strength, not your own. What are the areas of your life that you need to entrust to God's sovereignty?

 SNAPSHOTS

Moses: God used Moses to lead the Israelites out of Egypt, where they were slaves. Because of Pharaoh's hard heart, it took 10 plagues on Egypt to convince him to let the Israelites go. The tenth plague, on the firstborn, began the Hebrew tradition of celebrating the Passover.

Key Verse: "The Lord said, 'I have indeed seen the misery of My people in Egypt. I have heard them crying out because of their slave drivers, and I am concerned about their suffering' " (Exodus 3:7).

Etc.:   (Your own questions, comments, observations)

THE RISK
OF FREEDOM

(Exodus 13–19; 32–34)

It's a warm, sunny day—the kind of day that practically demands that you go for a drive. You gather your friends, throw together a picnic lunch, grab a Frisbee and some towels, and head for the beach. You're all in the car, listening to the radio and not paying much attention to anything other than enjoying the day, when suddenly a police car races up behind you with red lights flashing. How would you feel at that moment?

Someone has said that the only cars that don't slow down when near a police car are the ones that are parked. In the previous example, let's imagine the police car pulls around you and speeds off after some *real* felons. Even if you hadn't been speeding or doing anything wrong, it's still likely that your heart rate would be accelerated for a while and that you would need to use one of the beach towels to dry your sweating palms. The sudden "jerk back to reality" can be quite traumatic—even if it's only temporary and even if it's not your fault.

In this session, the Israelites are going to experience a similar sensation. But first we have to get them headed for the beach, so to speak. The last session was something of a cliff-hanger. After years of slavery, the Lord sent a leader to carry His people out of Egypt. And God's leader, Moses, faced some tough opposition. Only after 10 increasingly severe plagues would Pharaoh allow the Israelites to leave. But Moses stood his ground, and (with God's help, of course) eventually won the battle of the wills. The last session ended with the Israelites all abuzz about leaving Egypt.

JOURNEY ONWARD

Just like any other long trip, there were a number of last-minute preparations to attend to. But first on the list was a dedication ceremony. God had just spared the lives of all the firstborn male children and animals of those families which had put blood on the doorposts. Since these people (and animals) had lived, they were special to God. So the Lord told Moses to consecrate the firstborn males and commemorate the day the Israelites left Egypt. From this point on, the sacrifice of firstborn animals would be a remembrance to future generations of God's deliverance of His people from slavery (Exodus 13:14-16).

Sometimes we look for major signs from God that will prove His existence or His love for us. And in doing so, we often overlook the millions of little ways God shows His love. Read Exodus 13:17-18 and explain one of the "little" things God did because He cared for the Israelites.

Exodus 13:18 tells us that the Israelites were traveling "armed for battle." Perhaps they didn't have many weapons, but they were organized—not what you might expect for hundreds of thousands of slaves escaping from their masters. And they had a good reason to be confident about where they were going. Why? (13:21-22)

They were also carrying some unusual cargo. What was it? (13:19)

Meanwhile, back in Egypt, what was going on? (14:5-9)

What reaction did the Israelites have when they discovered Pharaoh's plans? (14:10-12)

Did God know what He was doing? How do you know? (14:1-4)

While the Israelites were panicking, did Moses have any doubts about God's ability to deliver them? (14:13-14)

Put yourself in the position of one of the Israelites. Your whole life has been spent doing what others tell you to do, and now you are suddenly free. But you and your friends have just discovered that freedom doesn't guarantee happiness. Trained armies and chariots are behind you. The Red Sea is in front of you. As far as you can see, you have no way out. How would you feel?

Apparently Pharaoh didn't want to kill the Israelites, because he was mourning the loss of their services (14:5). But all the Israelites could

see was a huge army fast approaching. While the Israelites were complaining, worrying, and wishing they were back in Egypt, Moses was
crying out to God (14:15). But God told Moses it was time everyone
moved on. Read Exodus 14:16-22 and answer the following questions.

What action did Moses take to part the waters of the Red Sea?

What action did God take to part the waters of the Red Sea?

How did God keep the Egyptian army from catching up with the
Israelites?

How were the Egyptian chariots slowed down? (14:23-25)

When the sea went back to its original state, how many Egyptians sur-
vived? (14:26-28)

What effect did this miracle have on the morale of the Israelites?
(14:29-31)

There was quite a victory celebration on the other side of the Red Sea.
In fact, Exodus 15:1-21 records a long song of praise and triumph sung
by the Israelites. But it didn't take long for their good feelings to wear
off. Read Exodus 15:22-25 and describe the problem.

Now read Exodus 15:25-27 and explain how the problem was resolved.

▌

Notice that if the Israelites had kept going without complaining, they would have seen that the Lord was taking them to a place with 12 springs and 70 palm trees. (It's not that God doesn't care about us, but often we aren't patient enough to see *how* God will take care of us.)

Almost as soon as the water crisis was solved, the Israelites began to complain about food (16:1-3). Again they began to long for the "good old days" of slavery in Egypt, where they could at least get a good meal once in a while. It seems that by this time the Israelites should have been learning to ask God for whatever they needed. But even though they were still grumbling, God decided to give them what they wanted. What did God promise to do for the Israelites, and why? (16:4-8)

▌

How did God fulfill His promise? (16:13-18)

▌

The gathering of bread was supposed to become a daily regimen. What happened if someone tried to stockpile a supply above what he needed? (16:19-20)

▌

Why do you think God didn't want people to gather more than a day's supply at a time?

▌

What was the exception to the "one-day's-supply-at-a-time" rule? (16:21-30)

▌

The people called the bread "manna," which in Hebrew means, "What is it?" What did manna taste like? (16:31)

▌

A small portion of manna was preserved by Moses (at God's command) to keep for future generations. God used manna to supply food for His people for 40 years, until they entered the land He had promised them (which contained an ample food supply).

You might think now that since the Israelites had a daily supply of food and the Lord was still going before them visibly (in a pillar of fire and pillar of cloud), and since He had performed great miracles for them (the plagues in Egypt, the parting of the Red Sea, etc.), that the people would relax a little and trust God to take care of them. No way. They again came to a spot where there was no water and immediately began complaining to Moses and giving him the same old we-never-should-have-left-Egypt speech (17:1-3). But Moses had learned to turn to God in any crisis, so that's exactly what he did. What instructions did God give Moses? (17:4-7)

▌

[NOTE: *Massah* means "testing," and *Meribah* means "quarreling."]

Not long afterward, the Israelites had problems of another kind. While they were camped, they were attacked by the Amalekites. But again, Moses knew just what to do. He put Joshua in charge of the Israelite army, while he took Aaron and Hur and went up on a hill that overlooked the battlefield. Whenever Moses lifted his hands (a symbol of appeal for God's help), the Israelites would win. But when he got tired and lowered his arms, the Amalekites would begin to win. How did Moses prevent his fatigue from interfering with the Israelite victory? (17:12-13)

▌

As God continued to direct the Israelites, they began to approach Mount Sinai. While in the area, Moses sent his wife and sons to visit

Jethro, his wife's father. Jethro returned to the Israelite camp with Moses' family, and he and Moses had a good talk and caught up on what had been happening. Jethro was pleased to hear of God's great protection and deliverance of His people, and he offered sacrifices to God.

The next day Jethro performed the services of a management consultant. Read Exodus 18:13-27 and answer the following questions.

What problem did Jethro observe?

What adjustment did Jethro suggest?

Exactly three months after the Israelites left Egypt, they reached Mount Sinai, a significant stopping-off place. For one thing, their arrival fulfilled the promise God had made Moses from the burning bush—that after Moses had brought the people out of Egypt he would worship God on the same mountain (3:12). But another significance of Mount Sinai was that it was a place to be set apart for God. It was there that God was going to meet with Moses. The Israelites were to consecrate themselves by washing their clothes (19:10) and abstaining from sexual relations (19:15). No one was to even touch the mountain. What was the penalty for disobedience? (19:12-13)

What were some of the signs that showed God was present on the top of the mountain? (19:16-19)

God then called Moses to the top of Mount Sinai to meet with Him. Read Exodus 32:1-6 and explain what was happening in the Israelite camp while Moses was gone.

God, of course, saw everything that was taking place at the foot of the mountain. He told Moses what was happening and made a suggestion to him. What did God suggest? (32:7-10)

Moses interceded for his people. What did he tell God in defense of the Israelites, and what effect did it have? (32:11-14)

So Moses returned to his people with a copy of the Ten Commandments in his hand. What was special about this copy of the laws of God? (32:15-16)

How did Moses react when he observed firsthand the wickedness of the Israelites? (32:17-20)

While Aaron made feeble excuses (32:22-24), the Israelites were running wild. Moses stood at the entrance of the camp and called for all the people who stood for the Lord to meet him there. The Levites gathered with him, and Moses sent them out to kill any rebellious Israelites they saw. Three thousand people died from the swords of the Levites. This may seem like harsh punishment, but it is not so severe when you consider that God had already suggested exterminating the entire nation. The deaths of those 3,000 people showed that even though the Israelites were God's people, God would not overlook their selfish, sinful actions. They were free from Egypt, but they were not free to do whatever they wanted. God had a purpose for them and a destination (the Promised Land). If they were to arrive at their destination and fulfill the promise God had made to Abraham, Isaac, and Jacob, they were going to have to learn to control their self-centered wishes and let God lead them. So after the people came to their senses and began to realize the severity of their sin, Moses interceded for them (32:30-34).

There was no mistaking that Moses was very close to God during this time. How did the Israelites know that Moses really knew what God wanted them to do? (33:7-11)

Moses wanted to be even closer to God, and asked to see more of His glory (33:18). What did God do for Moses then? (33:19-23)

God met with Moses again to replace the shattered tablets (34:1-5), and Moses took them back to the Israelites. How did the people respond to Moses? Why? (34:29-35)

JOURNEY INWARD

As you consider the background of the Israelites' first few weeks out of Egypt, consider also the **relationship between freedom and risk.** You probably have already come to the realization that freedom isn't free. Freedom requires letting go of a sure thing and grasping for something you're not so sure about. And the transition is not usually an easy one.

In case you didn't notice, the Israelites were fickle people. They praised God to the max as soon as they got out of Egypt, but the moment they hit a snag (the Red Sea), they started saying, "I knew we never should have left Egypt. I sure wish we were back there now." They were all for God after He got them across the Red Sea. But as soon as Moses was gone for a few days, they were ready to assemble their own do-it-yourself god kit (the golden calf).

But before you're too quick to criticize the faithfulness of the Israelites, perhaps you need to examine your own life. If you are a Christian, God has delivered you from the bondage of sin. But when you discovered that He wanted you to leave certain people or practices behind, you may have wished that things were "the way they used to be." What are some things that are hard for you to "leave behind"?

What can you do to make sure you keep moving ahead instead of looking back?

What are some of your golden calves (the idols that take your attention away from the real God)?

What kinds of freedom have you discovered since becoming a Christian?

What risks have you had to take because of your Christian freedom?

Like the Israelites, you will often discover that if you move ahead as you face obstacles, God will get you through the obstacles somehow.

He may not part any seas for you, but He can do things just as miraculous if you stop griping and start walking.

 SNAPSHOTS

Crossing of the Red Sea: After Moses led the Israelites out of Egypt, Pharaoh changed his mind and pursued them. When they came to the Red Sea, God parted the waters and the Israelites passed through on dry ground, with water on both sides. But when Pharaoh's army followed, the water covered them and they all drowned.

Mount Sinai: This was a place set apart for God where the people worshiped Him. God gave Moses the Ten Commandments there.

Key Verse: "Come before the Lord, for He has heard your grumbling" (Exodus 16:9).

Etc.: (Your own questions, comments, observations)

PUTTING TOGETHER THE GAME PLAN

(Exodus 20–40; Leviticus; Numbers 1–9; Deuteronomy)

- You can't stay out past 11:00 on school nights.
- You gotta do your homework before you go bowling with your friends.
- You can't car date until you're 16.
- You can't play on the school team unless you have at least a C average.
- No talking in church.
- Keep off the grass.
- No smoking.
- Shoplifters will be prosecuted.
- Speeders will be ticketed.
- Jaywalkers will be shot at dawn.

- Clipping toenails in public will result in a minimum 5-year sentence in a maximum-security prison.

OK, OK. The last two are only jokes. But doesn't it seem like there's a dumb rule to keep you from doing just about anything that's *fun?* You know what these comments are leading up to, don't you? The old "rules-are-for-your-own-good" speech? That if you didn't have rules everyone could just go around doing what he or she wanted to do, resulting in the fall of civilization as we know it? That you should be *proud* to follow the rules set for you—no questions asked?

Actually, those statements do contain *some* truth, but they are not always correct. Rules *should* have a reason for existing, but sometimes the reasons are forgotten while the rules remain. For instance:

- In Cambodia, it was once against the law to insult a rice plant.
- A Chicago law prohibits feeding whiskey to canines.
- In Omaha, Nebraska, it is illegal to burp or sneeze while in church.
- Florida law forbids a housewife to break more than three dishes a day.
- In Maine, it's illegal to walk down the street with your shoelaces untied.
- It's against the law in Kansas to eat rattlesnake meat in public.

(From *Boyd's Book of Odd Facts,* L.M. Boyd, Signet.)

Sometimes you may have good reasons to challenge rules that exist for no apparent purpose. But first you should try to identify the motive behind the rule—to look beyond the *what* in order to determine the *why.* This is especially true for biblical rules. While it is important to obey God's laws "because He says so," it's also important to try to discover God's purpose for giving the rule in the first place. You may be surprised at what you find.

JOURNEY ONWARD

In the last session, Moses had gone up Mount Sinai to speak to God. But even before Moses started up the mountain, God had given the

Israelites some rules: (1) Wash your clothes and prepare for My coming (Exodus 19:10-11); (2) Don't touch Mount Sinai or you will be put to death (19:12); and Moses had added the third rule, (3) Don't have sex for the next three days (19:15). When the Lord appeared three days later, every Israelite in the camp trembled. No doubt some of them had been grumbling about having to obey all the "dumb" rules (especially rule #3), but when they experienced the presence of the Lord, they discovered *why* they should have been preparing for His coming. Without adequate preparation, they would not be spiritually ready to have God visit their camp.

As God began to give Moses some guidelines to live by, He started with the big ones—those we've come to know as the Ten Commandments (Exodus 20:3-17). On the following chart, fill in each of the commandments and the reason *why* you think God gave that specific commandment.

	COMMANDMENT	PURPOSE
(1) 20:3		
(2) 20:4-6		
(3) 20:7		
(4) 20:8-11		
(5) 20:12		

(6) 20:13		
(7) 20:14		
(8) 20:15		
(9) 20:16		
(10) 20:17		

The Ten Commandments were given by God so the Israelite nation could function smoothly. Yet it's hard to imagine any society in which *all* these rules are followed by *everybody*. (And if a nation can't follow 10 basic rules, how are they supposed to react when the government adds speeding laws, pet registrations, disturbing the peace ordinances, etc.?)

Before moving on, notice the order of the Ten Commandments. The first four rules concern our relationship with God. The last six pertain to our relationships with each other. The priority is a good one. Only after we have a proper respect for and attitude toward God can we have genuinely caring attitudes toward each other.

Also remember the context in which the Ten Commandments were given. God didn't just have Moses hand out tent flap hangers or bookmarks with the commandments printed on them. Instead, God made His presence known with thunder, lightning, trumpet sounds, and smoke. The people were afraid, and God had a reason for provoking their fear. What was it? (20:18-21)

Much of the following section of the Old Testament contains specific rules: for social relationships, for the building of the tabernacle, for priestly service, and so forth. This session isn't going to attempt to cover the rest of Exodus, Leviticus, Numbers, and Deuteronomy in detail, but it will give you a sampling of the rules given by God and the reasons behind many of them.

Match the people below with the rule he or she might be glad to have.

PERSON	RULE
A. A widow or orphan	_____ Exodus 21:2-3
B. A husband who suspects his wife of cheating on him	_____ Exodus 22:16-17
C. A male Hebrew slave	_____ Exodus 22:22-24
D. A poor person	_____ Exodus 23:9
E. A debtor	_____ Exodus 23:10-11 Deuteronomy 15:7-8
F. A girl seduced by a man to have sex	_____ Numbers 5:11-31
G. A person who accidentally kills someone else	_____ Deuteronomy 4:41-43
H. A foreigner in Israel	_____ Deuteronomy 15:1-6

How well would you have gotten along in Israelite society? Read each of the following laws and give yourself a grade for how well you obey each one.

Exodus 21:15 ___	Leviticus 19:18 ___
Exodus 21:17 ___	Leviticus 19:32 ___
Exodus 23:1 ___	Leviticus 24:10-16, 23 ___
Exodus 23:5 ___	Leviticus 27:30 ___
Leviticus 19:14 ___	Deuteronomy 21:18-21 ___

God also gave His people precise instructions pertaining to the exact setup and furnishings for the tabernacle, which the Israelites were to construct for worship. Read the following passages in Exodus, and above each reference try to draw the item described, or describe it in your own words.

Ark of the covenant (25:10-22)	Table for the bread of the Presence (25:23-30)
Lampstand (25:31-40)	Altar of burnt offering (27:1-8)
Altar of incense (30:1-10)	Basin (30:17-20)

The following is a floor plan of the tabernacle. Try to match the items you have drawn with their appropriate locations in the tabernacle. (See Exodus 26:34-35; 30:6, 18.)

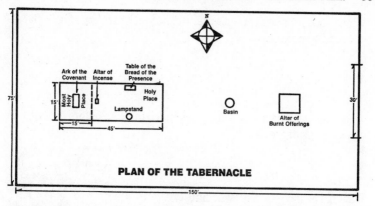

PLAN OF THE TABERNACLE

Notice that the instruments located near the holy of holies (where God was to reside) were of gold, while those farther away (in the outer court) were bronze. God's presence was given recognition and honor even in the design of the tabernacle. As the Israelites entered the courtyard of the tabernacle, they first came to the altar of burnt offering. There the priests could offer the sacrifices the people brought. The people were also able to see the bronze basin, where the priests would wash themselves before entering the holy place. But that's all that the normal people could see. Only the priests could enter the holy place, where the candlestick, table for the bread of the Presence, and the altar of incense were located.

And the priests also had to follow certain procedures as they came before God. In fact, even though Aaron was the high priest, two of his sons once brought an offering to the Lord in an improper way, and God killed them with fire (Leviticus 10:1-3). If God's punishment of them seems harsh, it is because He wanted to teach His people that there is a proper and an improper way to come before Him. The deaths of Aaron's sons would always be a solemn reminder to the Israelites that to ignore the holiness of God and come before Him in an uncaring or hypocritical manner is a sin which God detests.

Another procedure which highlighted the vast differences between man's sinfulness and God's holiness was the annual Day of Atonement. The instructions regarding the Day of Atonement are given in Leviticus 16. Read through the chapter, and as you do, answer the following questions.

Why couldn't the high priest enter the holy of holies (most holy place) any time he wanted to? (v. 2)

What preparations did the high priest have to make before entering the most holy place? (v. 4)

What did he have to take with him? (vv. 3, 5)

Why was the bull sacrificed? (vv. 6, 11)

What did the high priest do with the goats? (vv. 7-10)

How was he to respect the presence of the Lord (above the ark of the covenant)? (vv. 12-13)

After the high priest sacrificed the bull for his own sins (and those of his family) and sacrificed one goat for the sins of the Israelites, what was he to do with the other goat? (vv. 20-22)

How were the Israelites to respect the Day of Atonement? (vv. 29-31)

▌

What was the significance of the Day of Atonement? (v. 34)

▌

The **sin offering** made on the Day of Atonement was only one of several kinds of offerings practiced by the Israelites. Most of them are described in Leviticus 1–7:

- **Burnt offering** (Leviticus 1; 6:8-13)—A bull, ram, or bird was brought voluntarily to atone for an unintentional sin or to renew a commitment to the Lord.

- **Grain offering** (Leviticus 2; 6:14-23)—Grain, oil, flour, incense, or baked cakes or wafers (with salt) were offered voluntarily in recognition of the regular provisions of God for His people.

- **Fellowship offering** (Leviticus 3; 7:11-34)—An unblemished animal or unleavened bread, presented voluntarily and with an attitude of thanksgiving. This offering was usually accompanied by a group meal.

- **Sin offering** (Leviticus 4–5:13; 6:24-30)—A required sacrifice whenever someone sinned unintentionally. The offering depended on the economic status of the person and the scope of the offering (whether for an individual or the entire nation).

- **Guilt offering** (Leviticus 5:14–6:7; 7:1-6)—Another required sacrifice to atone for any sins that needed restitution. In addition to asking for God's forgiveness, the person making the sacrifice would make right his wrong (to another person) and pay an additional fifth of his injury as a fine. This offering was made in cases of cheating, lying, extortion, etc.

But Hebrew life wasn't all solemnn. Interspersed with the holy days were a variety of feasts: the Feast of Weeks, the Feast of Trumpets, and the Feast of Tabernacles, to name a few (Leviticus 23).

Before we complete this session on rules, a few additional laws should be considered. The Israelites were expected to eat only certain "clean" foods. They were to avoid "unclean" foods. How did they know which animals and fish were OK to eat and which ones were to be avoided? (Deuteronomy 14:3-8)

What were some of the birds to be avoided? (Deuteronomy 14:11-19)

Finally, it needs to be pointed out that God did not intend for anyone to use His laws for unjust personal gain. Several of the laws given to Moses concerned the people who were poor, slaves, or underprivileged in other ways. Read each of the following laws and explain how they were meant to benefit someone who might be going through tough times.

- Deuteronomy 15:1-11

- Deuteronomy 15:12-18

- Deuteronomy 19:1-7

- Leviticus 23:22

Finally, read Exodus 23:20-33. What promises did God make if the people would obey Him?

JOURNEY INWARD

This session by no means covers all the laws, feasts, ceremonies, and other social guidelines listed in the Old Testament. But hopefully it is enough to let you see that God had a purpose behind His **rules and regulations.** His laws were given out of the love He had for His people. They weren't a bunch of "dumb" rules from the mouth of an authoritarian dictator. They were more like a game plan from a Coach who wanted to see His "team" succeed.

God knew the Israelites could exist only with a system of order and discipline. Yet many times critics of the Bible like to pull an Old Testament law out of context to illustrate how "cruel" God is. For instance, suppose a friend says: "The Bible says in Exodus 21:23-25, 'If there is serious injury, you are to take life for life, eye for eye, tooth for tooth, hand for hand, foot for foot, burn for burn, wound for wound, bruise for bruise.' I thought the Bible taught forgiveness, not revenge." How would you respond?

What are some of the rules in the Bible that make you wonder why you should obey them?

What are other rules that you tend to question:

- From parents?

- From teachers?

- From church leaders?

● From your boss(es) at work?

Now go back through your list of questionable rules and try to think *why* they exist. If you can't figure it out on your own, take your questions to a pastor, youth leader, or Sunday School teacher and discuss them.

Conclude this session by reading 2 Timothy 3:16-17. How do these verses relate to your list of "questionable" rules?

 SNAPSHOTS

Ten Commandments:	God gave Moses the Ten Commandments to give to the Israelites.
Key Verse:	"I am the Lord your God. . . . You shall have no other gods before Me. You shall not make for yourself an idol. . . . You shall not misuse the name of the Lord your God. . . . Observe the Sabbath day by keeping it holy. . . . Honor your father and your mother. . . . You shall not murder. You shall not commit adultery. You shall not steal. You shall not give false testimony against your neighbor. You shall not covet your neighbor's wife" (Deuteronomy 5:6-21).
Etc.:	(Your own questions, comments, observations)

ARE WE THERE YET?

(Numbers 9–36)

Have you ever been on a vacation that starts out great, but everyone's patience eventually gets pushed to the limit? For the first few hours everything is fine—you're all telling jokes, singing, watching the scenery, and really enjoying each other's company.

But after a while you run out of jokes and songs. The scenery all starts to look the same. The sun comes out and it gets *hot*. Your little sister falls asleep on *your* side of the car. And before long, you're at each other's throats. Sanity disappears and is replaced by whining. And complaining! Dad is threatening to pull the car over to the side of the road. Mom is telling little sister (who has finally woken up) that she's not really carsick. And Sis is proving Mom wrong—all over the back of the car.

Or maybe you've been on a camping trip or retreat where everything is just *perfect*. You even stay up all night so you can talk and enjoy the terrific feeling. But the next day your friends don't seem as wonderful as they did the night before, and your nerves stay a little frazzled until you catch up on your sleep.

Sometimes even the best intentions get fouled up by stress, fatigue, or other less-than-ideal circumstances. Such is the case in this session. In session 7 we left the Israelites at the foot of Mount Sinai as Moses went up to receive the laws of God. The last session allowed you to examine several of those laws. Now it's time for the Israelites to move on toward the Promised Land.

JOURNEY ONWARD

A year had passed since the Israelites left Egypt, so it was again time for the Israelites to celebrate the Passover. But the anticipation of Passover caused problems for some of the people. Why? (Numbers 9:4-7)

What distinctions did God make concerning who could and couldn't celebrate Passover without severe consequences? (9:8-10, 13)

About a month after the Passover commemoration at Sinai, God let the Israelites know it was time to move on. How could they tell it was time to go? (9:15-23)

The journey had hardly begun when the people began to complain about the hardships. What happened because of their complaining? (11:1)

What did Moses do, and what happened? (11:2-3)

How long had it been since the people had worshiped at Sinai? (10:33)

A year in the desert had made most of the Israelites pretty cranky. As soon as Moses took care of one crisis, the people began to gripe about their diet. It wasn't enough that God was producing food (manna) from nowhere to feed 600,000 men (plus women and children) *every day*. The Israelites wanted variety. What foods were they craving? (11:4-6)

This time even Moses was ready to give up on the Israelites. He accused God of expecting him to baby-sit, so to speak. (See Numbers 11:11-12.) Moses saw no way to supply meat for the people to eat, even if they slaughtered all their animals (11:21-22). Letting the complaints get to him, Moses even told God to kill him if God wasn't going to do anything (11:15). So God responded in two ways. What was the first thing God did? (11:16-17)

Then what did God do? (11:18-20, 31-32)

Notice the people's reaction to God's provision for their desires. They had been complaining about a lack of meat, so God sent it to them in massive amounts. But was anyone down at the tabernacle conducting a thanksgiving service? No! They were all out hogging as many of the quail as they could gather. God was angry at the greedy, disrespectful attitudes of the people. What did He do? (11:33-34)

It seems that the complaining nature of the Israelite people was contagious—even their leaders were catching the "disease." Miriam and Aaron began to gossip about Moses one day. They *said* it was because they disapproved of his wife, but it appears there was a more truthful reason. What was it, and were their complaints valid? (12:1-3)

What did God do to silence Miriam and Aaron's complaining? (12:4-15)

But after all the aggravation and complaining, the Israelites finally arrived in the area of their final destination—the Promised Land. God had brought them safely from Egypt. He had put up with their whining and stubbornness. He had provided for them in numerous situations that seemed hopeless. And finally the Israelites stood on the outskirts of Canaan.

SPYING OUT THE LAND
Moses selected one person from each tribe to go ahead and explore the land. What were some of the things the 12 spies were supposed to check out? (13:17-20)

The spies were gone 40 days and then returned to camp with a report and some samples of Canaan's produce. What report did the spies bring back, and what advice did the majority of them give? (13:26-33)

The Israelites' response to the spies' report was the usual one—complaining. They grumbled against Moses and Aaron as usual, and this time they even started to look for a new leader who would take them back to Egypt (14:1-4). But two of the spies, Joshua and Caleb, interrupted and voiced a minority opinion. What advice did they give the Israelites? (14:5-9)

The advice of Joshua and Caleb was not well received. In fact, the people were ready to stone them. What stopped the stoning ceremony? (14:10)

God was angry. (Don't you think He had every right to be?) He again suggested that Moses might be a lot better off if God just wiped out the Israelites and started a new nation of people. But Moses again interceded for the Israelites—not in defense of their actions, but in defense of their reputation as God's people. Moses realized that God could not break His previous promise to Abraham, Isaac, and Jacob to establish a nation of their descendants. He also knew that if God wiped out the Israelites, the Egyptians and other heathen nations would not understand a God who rescued His people only to kill them Himself. So Moses asked God to forgive the Israelites.

God granted Moses' request, but He knew that this generation of people was not ready to receive the challenge or the blessings of entering

the Promised Land. What did God tell Moses to say to the Israelites?
(14:20-35)

Who were the exceptions to God's decree? (14:30)

What happened to the 10 fearful spies? (14:36-38)

How long would it be before the nation of Israel could enter Canaan?
(14:34-35)

When Moses told the people what God had said, they were first very
sad. But then they decided to ignore God's instructions and invade the
land of Canaan on their own. Moses tried to persuade them not to do
so, but they wouldn't listen to him. What was the result of their efforts
to take the Promised Land by their own power? (14:39-45)

Even though the Israelites learned the hard way that they couldn't enter Canaan during their lifetime, God assured Moses that it would happen eventually. In fact, Numbers 15 contains several instructions given
Moses to observe 40 years later when the Israelites would finally go
into the Promised Land. God made it clear that unintentional sins could
be confessed and forgiven. But people who had no respect for God and
sinned intentionally would be severely judged.

REBELLION IN THE RANKS

A case of intentional sin is recorded in Numbers 16. A man named Korah and about 250 other people decided to stand in opposition to the leadership of Moses and Aaron. Many of these people were leaders with important roles in the care and keeping of the tabernacle, and had a spiritual commitment to the Israelite community. But apparently they felt they weren't receiving proper recognition for what they were doing. They approached Moses and Aaron and said in effect, "We're all important to God. Why do you two think you're so great?" (16:1-3)

Moses was upset when he heard Korah's accusations, but he decided to let God settle the matter. He told Korah and his supporters to prepare fire and incense in their censers (ceremonial bronze containers for burning incense to God) and offer it to the Lord. The person God chose would be His intended leader. The next morning when the preparations were made, Moses separated Korah and two other ringleaders (Dathan and Abiram—see 16:12-14) from the rest of the group. What happened to them and to the rest of the 250 rebels? (16:25-35)

God then had Eleazar, the son of Aaron and a true priest, collect the censers and convert them into sheets of bronze with which to overlay the altar. From that point on, every time an Israelite saw the bronze overlay on the altar, he or she would be reminded of God's designation that only descendants of Aaron could burn incense before Him.

You would think that the people of Israel would catch on that God didn't like them to question His wisdom choosing leaders. But *the very next day* the whole Israelite community came out and accused Moses and Aaron of killing God's people. God again suggested that He destroy all the Israelites and start over with Moses and Aaron, and Moses and Aaron again prayed on behalf of their nation. However, God did send a plague among the people, and Aaron (as priest) was the appropriate person to make atonement for the people and stop it. He immediately offered incense, but almost 15,000 people died before the plague was stopped. (See Numbers 16:41-50.)

God provided another sign so everyone would know that Aaron was His appointed priest. What was the test, and what was the result of the test? (17:1-9)

Not too much of the Israelites' 40 years of wandering through the wilderness is detailed. But apparently Numbers 20 describes events of the last year. (The chapter refers to the death of Aaron, and Numbers 33:38 tells us that Aaron died in the fortieth year after the Israelites left Egypt.) Things weren't all that different in the fortieth year than what you've seen so far. The people were in a place without water, and they gathered together to complain to Moses and Aaron. The two leaders consulted God. What did God tell Moses to do? (20:7-8)

What did Moses do instead, and what was the result of Moses' disobedience? (20:9-12)

Soon afterward, God told Moses and Aaron to ascend Mount Hor because Aaron was going to die there. Eleazar, Aaron's son, then became high priest. And in spite of the opposition Aaron had received in the past, the whole nation mourned his death for 30 days (20:22-29).

But the people were still complainers. They were voicing the same old gripes—no water, rotten food, and a desire to return to Egypt. This time God sent poisonous snakes into the camp and many people died from their bites. The Israelites quickly repented, asking Moses to tell God to take away the snakes. What was God's solution? (21:8-9)

CLASH OF NATIONS

While traveling through the desert, the Israelites had regular encounters with other nations. Sometimes they would ask permission to travel through someone's land with the promise they would not harm anything. Other times they would stand and fight. And by following God's instructions, they were successful in their battles. (See Numbers 20:19-21; 21:1-3, 23-25, 31-35.)

So when the Israelites camped near Moab, Balak the king became worried about what might happen. He sent for a man named Balaam who was known for being able to bestow blessings or curses with remarkable results. It is debated whether Balaam was a prophet of the true God or a "free-lance" prophet for a number of gods. But God appeared to him with a message. What was it? (22:12)

God's first instructions to Balaam were not to go to King Balak at all. But when the Moabite king sent a second group of messengers to Balaam, God told Balaam to go with them—with the condition that Balaam do only what God said to do. And Balaam's journey to Moab has to be one of the most remarkable in history. What happened that was so unusual? (22:21-35)

Balak expected Balaam to curse the Israelites upon reaching Moab, but Balaam blessed them instead (23:1-12). Balak decided to try again, and took Balaam to another location. But he again blessed Israel. Balak told Balaam if he wasn't going to curse the Israelites, not to say anything at all. Balaam replied that he had to do what God told him to do (23:13-26). Balak tried a third time (and at a third location), but Balaam again blessed Israel. In disgust, Balak sent Balaam home (23:27–24:25).

Balaam refused to compromise what God had told him, but the Israelites continued to find new ways to reject God. While in the area of Moab, the Hebrew men started to fool around with the Moabite women. They also participated in the Moabite religious ceremonies, feasting and worshiping false gods.

God said that the guilty people must be put to death. He had Moses and Israel's judges carry out the punishment, but He also sent a plague among the people. What stopped this plague? (25:6-9)

After the 24,000 people died in the plague, God told Moses and Eleazar to take a count of the people by families. The total number of men in Israel was 601,730 (26:51). So in spite of all the hardships and setbacks during Israel's desert wanderings, their numerical strength had not dwindled (see Exodus 12:37). This census was taken in preparation to divide the Promised Land by tribes. How many people were still living who had been included in the census 40 years before? (26:64-65)

God also wanted to prepare a leader to follow Moses. Who was to be the next leader of Israel? (27:15-21)

But God wasn't through with Moses just yet. At God's command, Moses organized a war against the Midianites, who had been part of the cause of the spiritual sins committed by the Israelites. The Israelites were victorious and divided the spoils (Numbers 31). Moses also took care of preparing the settlement of the tribes in Canaan. He made sure the Levites would be provided for and established cities of refuge where people guilty of unintentional manslaughter could go for protection (Numbers 32–36).

Moses then called Joshua and gave him a challenge in front of the Israelites. What promises were included in Moses' challenge to Joshua? (Deuteronomy 31:7-8)

Read Deuteronomy 34 and describe the death of Moses—the circumstances, his age, his physical condition, and so forth. Do you think this was a fearful time for Moses?

JOURNEY INWARD

You might think the main theme of this session would be complaining (and it *is* a topic that should be considered). But the greater theme is the certainty of **God's promises.** In spite of the Israelites' complaints, God still delivered His people to the Promised Land—just as He promised He would.

Let's start by examining the issue of complaining in your life. For instance, how do you respond when a parent gives you a list of chores to do before you can go out with your friends? When a brother or sister borrows something of yours without asking? When a teacher loads you down with repetitive homework? These situations *can* help you develop responsibility, patience, and wisdom—but only if you let them. You see, if complaining becomes a way of life for you, you will resist growth and end up with bitterness and hurt feelings instead of a list of positive qualities. And then, of course, if complaining becomes an automatic response to the difficulties of life, you will miss the joy of meeting the many, many challenges that God provides for your growth.

Think of the past week and list all the instances you can remember when you complained about something. Make a note of each instance below. (Take the time to list *all* of them.)

After reviewing your list of complaints, ask yourself, "Am I becoming a chronic (regular) complainer?" And if the answer is yes, ask yourself, "Do I want to go on this way, or do something now to change my attitude?"

That's where God's faithfulness in keeping His promises comes in. What biblical promises can you claim that would help you cut down on your tendency to complain? (For instance, Philippians 4:13 says, "I can do everything through Him [Jesus] who gives me strength.") God will honor *all* His promises, but you need to know what they are so you can count on Him in times of crisis.

In spite of the griping and whining of the Israelites, God didn't go back on His commitment to make a nation of Abraham's descendants. It's not that God suffered because His people were so stubborn, but the Israelites certainly lost out on many blessings God could have given them. What are some things you might be missing out on by complaining too much?

Notice a few other things about this session. First, God's timing is as important as God's will. It was God's *will* for the Israelites to enter the Promised Land, but they tried to enter (the first time) after God told them it was no longer the right *time*. Second, notice that as much as the Israelites complained about *their* journey and *their* struggles, it was *God* who was getting them there. And third, notice that God expects obedience from *all* His people—no exceptions. Even Moses, after all the times he was faithful when no one else seemed to be, had to accept God's chastisement for disobedience (striking the stone instead of speaking to it).

Spend a few minutes now thinking about the times you have been guilty of sins as severe as those the Israelites committed. Ask God's forgiveness for the past, and ask Him to prepare you to handle similar future situations that are sure to arise.

SNAPSHOTS

Wandering in the Wilderness:	After leaving Mount Sinai, the Lord led the people through the wilderness in a pillar of fire by night and a cloud by day.
Spies in Canaan:	Moses sent one person from each tribe to explore Canaan. Ten spies were afraid to enter the land, but two believed the Lord would give it to them.
Key Verse:	"The Lord is slow to anger, abounding in love and forgiving sin and rebellion. Yet He does not leave the guilty unpunished" (Numbers 14:18).
Etc.:	(Your own questions, comments, observations)

OVER THE RIVER AND THROUGH THE CITIES

(Book of Joshua)

Have you ever bought something which came with a rebate offer? You fill out a coupon, attach it to your sales receipt and proof of purchase, and you get money back. But the offer is good *only if you mail it in*. You can collect all the required elements to receive the rebate, and you can address and stamp the envelope. But if you don't walk it to the mailbox, you won't receive what you are entitled to.

JOURNEY ONWARD

As the Israelites prepared to enter the Promised Land, they received a similar offer. What promise did God make Joshua about how much the Israelites would receive? (Joshua 1:1-5)

What conditions did Joshua have to fulfill in order for God to keep His promise? (1:6-9)

This time the Israelites planned to enter the Promised Land at a different point than they had 40 years earlier. On the map below you will see where they were going to enter each time. This time they were going to cross the Jordan River to enter Canaan. Actually, two and a half tribes didn't really want to cross the river to settle. The tribes of Reuben and Gad, and half the tribe of Manasseh, had large herds and flocks. They wanted to settle where they were—on the eastern side of the Jordan River. They had previously asked Moses if they could stay there. What arrangement did Moses make with them? (Numbers 32:1-6, 16-22)

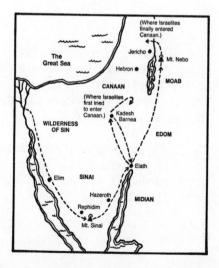

Joshua honored the agreement the two and a half tribes had made with Moses, and those tribes gave Joshua all the respect that they had given Moses (Joshua 1:12-18). In fact, a new spirit of hope seems to be present in the first few chapters of Joshua. The desert wanderings seem to have inspired the people to move forward and take the land this time. But Joshua wasn't too hasty. He sent two spies ahead to check out the first big obstacle in their path—the enormous city of Jericho. Read Joshua 2 and answer the following questions.

Who did the spies meet in Jericho who took care of them?

What was the attitude of the people of Jericho toward Israel?

What agreement did the spies make with their secret ally in Jericho?

What signal did the two parties agree on?

The spies returned and gave a positive report to Joshua. The Israelites immediately prepared to move toward Jericho. As they marched, the Levites carried the ark of the covenant in the front of the procession. The rest of the assembly followed at a distance, showing respect for the symbolic presence of God.

The Lord wanted Joshua to be a confident leader with the assurance that God could get him through any crisis. So God arranged for a spectacular crossing of the Jordan River. What happened as the Israelites prepared to go across? (3:14-17)

God had told Joshua to select 12 men—one from each tribe. What did these men do as the Israelites crossed the Jordan? (4:1-7)

When the U.S. astronauts went to the moon, some of the "souvenirs" they brought back were moon rocks. The stones didn't look much different than earth rocks, but they were significant because of where they had been. The stones selected by Joshua's volunteers were also ordinary rocks, but the fact that they had been picked up from the dry bed of the Jordan River during flood stage made them significant. They were to be piled up as a memorial to Israelites forever. What effect did the Jordan River crossing have on the people's attitude toward Joshua's leadership ability? (4:14)

While the spectacular Jordan River crossing may have bolstered Joshua's confidence as a leader, it totally demoralized the Canaanite leaders. The word of the crossing spread quickly, and the inhabitants of Canaan were quaking in their sandals.

But God wasn't quite ready to lead His people into battle. The practice of circumcising eight-day-old babies had been discontinued during the 40 years of wandering in the desert. Consequently, a generation of Israelites had grown up without the identifying mark that they were God's people (see Genesis 17:9-14). So before the nation of Israel marched in to claim God's promise to them, Joshua circumcised all the males.

It was also time for the annual Passover ceremony, which too had been discontinued during their desert wanderings. And the day after the Israelites celebrated the Passover, a custom they had practiced for the past 40 years was discontinued. What was the habit and why was it done away with at this particular time? (5:10-12)

JERICHO FALLS

As the Israelites approached the city of Jericho, Joshua received a visit from an unusual guest. Read Joshua 5:13–6:5 and answer the following questions.

Who was Joshua's visitor?

What did he tell Joshua to do?

What were his instructions for attacking Jericho?

Joshua did as his visitor had instructed for the first six days. And on the seventh day, just as the Israelites prepared to overtake the city, Joshua gave a couple of additional, specific instructions. One command concerned Rahab and her family. The other referred to the valuable possessions within the city. What were Joshua's instructions regarding these things? (6:17-19)

How did the Israelites get inside the massive walls of Jericho? (6:20)

How many fighting men did Israel have? (4:13)

With all those soldiers, why do you think God gave the instructions He did for entering Jericho?

Before moving on, Joshua placed a curse on the ruins of Jericho. What was the curse? (6:26)

I

(This curse will come up again in Book 2 of the BibleLog series, *That's the Way the Kingdom Crumbles.*)

The Israelites were feeling pretty good after the victory God had given them. Jericho had been a massive, awesome city. The next one they had to face, Ai, was wimpy in comparison. Joshua sent spies ahead, and they came back and told most of the army to take the day off. The spies supposed that two or three thousand men would be all it would take to defeat Ai. What happened during the battle? (7:3-5)

I

What effect did the battle have on the Israelites?

I

Joshua was crushed. He spent the day face down before the ark, praying to the Lord. He knew how the word had spread about Israel's triumphs. He also knew that word of their defeat would spread just as quickly, and he feared what would happen if the Canaanite kings got together and decided to attack Israel. Then God told Joshua what the problem was. Why had the Israelites been defeated? (7:10-13)

I

The next day the Israelites presented themselves before God. By casting lots, God singled out the tribe that was guilty. He narrowed it down to the clan and then the family. Finally, the guilty person was selected—a man named Achan. After going through all this ceremony, Achan confessed. What had he done in disobedience to God's instructions? (7:20-21)

I

Joshua sent people to confirm Achan's story, and it checked out. What was Achan's punishment for his sin? (7:24-26)

■

After Achan's sin had been revealed and punished, the Israelites again had God's blessing and turned their attention back to the city of Ai. (It's ironic that Achan didn't obey God just once, because this time God gave the Israelites permission to keep the goods and livestock of the city they were attacking [8:1-2].) Joshua had a good strategy to take over Ai. What was his plan? (8:3-8)

■

Joshua's plan worked wonderfully. As the men of Ai went rushing after the men who were with Joshua, the other Israelites came out of hiding and set the city on fire. Then the two groups of Israelites sandwiched the men of Ai between them and completely wiped them out (8:9-28).

Joshua wasn't the kind of leader who let these victories go to his head. After the Israelites defeated Ai, he built an altar to God. All of Israel assembled there, and Joshua read them all the laws that God had given Moses. As they entered the Promised Land, Joshua wanted them to be reminded of the instructions as well as the promises of God.

ISRAEL DECEIVED
The news of Israel's victories was spreading through the land of Canaan. Many of the kings in the area began to unite and form a coalition to fight against Israel. But the people of one area, Gibeon, came up with a different strategy to confront the Israelites. What did the Gibeonites do to avoid being killed by the people of Israel? (9:3-15)

■

Three days later the Israelites discovered that the cities of Gibeon were nearby, so they went there. They were annoyed at the Gibeon-ites' deception, but since Israel had sworn an oath of allegiance to Gibe-on, they couldn't attack. Why hadn't Israel seen through the deceit of the Gibeonites? (9:14)

What did they do instead of wiping out the cities of Gibeon? (9:20-27)

The coalition of Canaanite kings had been hoping to recruit the Gibeon-ites to fight with them, and were dismayed to discover that Gibeon had joined forces with Israel. Gibeon was a large city with many good fight-ers, so five kings united to attack Gibeon. The Gibeonites quickly sent word to Joshua, asking for his help. God assured Joshua of another vic-tory, and was true to His word. After Joshua's best men marched all night to pull a surprise attack on the Canaanite kings, what were a cou-ple of things God did to help the Israelites win? (10:7-14)

As Canaanite armies fled from the Israelites, the five kings hid in a cave. Joshua had his people roll stones across the entrance to the cave and post a small guard, while the rest of his army chased down the Ca-naanite armies before they reached their cities. Only a few Canaanites made it back safely. Then Joshua had the five kings taken out of the cave and killed. Their bodies were then thrown back into the cave, which became their tomb.

DIVIDING THE LAND

Joshua turned his attention to the southern cities of Canaan and defeat-ed them all. Then he moved north and defeated those cities, even though they had large numbers of horses and chariots. With the excep-tion of the people of Gibeon, the Israelites defeated every city they encountered (11:19). With the major wars over, Joshua divided the territory and gave each tribe an inheritance to conquer and settle. On the following map you can see where each tribe settled.

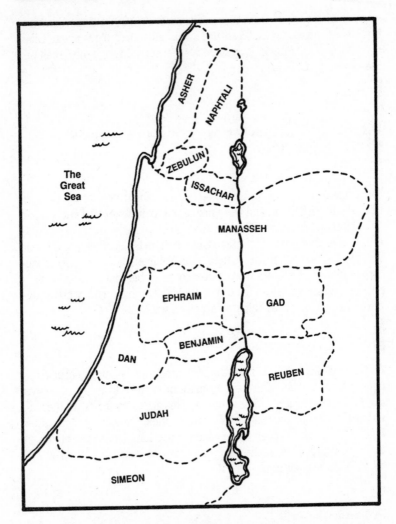

As you look at the map, notice a couple of things. First, you probably remember that Jacob had 12 sons, and 12 tribes settled in this area, but two of the names don't match. Jacob's sons included Levi and Joseph, but you won't find either of those names on the map. The Levites didn't receive a geographic area of the Promised Land because they were to take care of the things of God (Deuteronomy 18:1-2; Joshua 13:14). Instead they were given cities located throughout the land of Canaan, and their needs were supplied by offerings given from the other tribes (Joshua 21). Joseph isn't listed because his inheritance was passed on to his two sons, Ephraim and Manasseh. So the tribes that settled in the Promised Land were the descendants of the 12 sons of Jacob minus Levi and Joseph, plus Ephraim and Manasseh.

Second, the tribes of Gad, Reuben, and half the tribe of Manasseh settled in the land east of the Jordan River which Moses had promised them. They fulfilled their promise to Moses, helped the other Israelites defeat the Canaanites, and returned home with Joshua's blessing (Joshua 22:1-8). But their distinctive geographic location caused them some problems.

Just before they crossed the Jordan on their way home, they built a large altar beside the river. The other Israelites assumed that the two and a half tribes were rejecting the altar at the tabernacle and separating themselves from Israel. The nine and a half tribes even prepared to go to war against the two and a half tribes. But before they did, they sent Phinehas (the son of Eleazar, the priest) and a representative from each of the ten tribes to see what the other tribes had to say for themselves. What reason did the two and a half tribes give for building the altar? (22:21-29)

Their answer satisfied Phinehas and the delegation from Israel, so they all returned home and a war was avoided.

Joshua and Caleb received special inheritances in the land of Canaan. (They should have. If Israel had listened to them instead of the other 10 spies, they all could have settled in the Promised Land 40 years earlier.) Also, the cities of refuge that God had previously designated through Moses were set up throughout the Promised Land at this time.

Even though Joshua designated the inheritances for each of the tribes, not quite all of the fighting was over. Joshua left it up to each tribe to run out the rest of the Canaanites in its territory. (For example, see Joshua 17:17-18.)

Before Joshua died, he called together the leaders of Israel and gave them a promise and a warning. What was the promise? (23:3-5)

What was the warning? (23:12-13)

Then he assembled all the tribes at Shechem to review the story of how God had given them the land of Canaan. God reminded the people of the covenant He had made with them, and Joshua urged them to renew it. Read Joshua 24:14-27. What did the people choose to do?

Not long afterward, Joshua died at 110 years of age. Eleazar the high priest (Aaron's son) also died, and Phinehas, his son, received his inheritance. And one final bit of unfinished business was taken care of during Joshua's term of leadership. What was it? (Joshua 24:32, and review Genesis 50:25)

JOURNEY INWARD

The events in this session can teach us a lot about how to handle **problems.** Jericho was a massive, seemingly unbeatable problem. But by following God's simple instructions, the problem self-destructed and Joshua didn't have to struggle with it at all. Ai should have been an easy problem to beat, but one person's unconfessed sin prevented Joshua (and the entire nation) from having victory over it. Gibeon was a problem that should have been demolished just like the others. But a hasty compromise meant that Joshua and the Israelites had to learn to live with the problem the rest of their lives. And finally, the tribes of Israel almost went to war between themselves because of a misunderstanding. Their problem was lack of communication. Think of the problems you face, and list them in the proper categories below.

Jericho Problems—Those massive problems that you will never defeat without God's help.

Ai Problems—Problems you face because your relationship with God is not quite where it should be.

Gibeon Problems—Problems you have because you compromise rather than taking a firm stand with other people.

Needless Problems—The situations that would probably clear themselves up if you communicated a little better.

Be assured that God can help you with any problem you have. Perhaps you noticed as you read through passages in Joshua that God often speaks in the past tense concerning events that haven't occurred yet. In verses such as Joshua 8:1 and 10:8, God tells Joshua, "I *have given* you victory in the battle that you will fight tomorrow." There is no doubt that *God* will give you victory over your problems as long as *you* give Him your obedience and trust.

One way to strengthen your trust in God is to remember the things He has done in the past. Just as God had the Israelites build a memorial from stones gathered from the dried up Jordan River, you have the opportunity to build your own memorial below. On each of the stones, write something that God has done for you in the past, or is doing for you every day. Then when you face large problems in the future, look back to this memorial and remember that God has been active in your life for a long time.

 SNAPSHOTS

Jericho: Joshua led the people to take the city of Jericho, according to the Lord's instructions to march around the city and shout at the sound of the trumpets.

Land Division: Joshua divided the territory among each tribe. They were told to conquer the remaining cities and settle in the land.

Key Verse: "Choose for yourselves this day whom you will serve. . . . But as for me and my household, we will serve the Lord" (Joshua 24:15).

Etc.:   (Your own questions, comments, observations)

TELL IT TO THE JUDGE

(Judges 1–12)

If you have a moldy orange in your refrigerator crisper, do you try to make it better by surrounding it with fresh new ones?

If you see a pile of rat poison on top of your pancakes, do you plop down a couple more pancakes to dilute the effect the poison will have on your body?

If your shiny new Ferrari gets a dime-sized speck of rust on the door, do you ignore the rust and hope it will disappear?

If your dentist says you have a small cavity, do you have him drill a few more small holes in the tooth so the first one won't be so conspicuous?

Obviously, the answer to all these questions is no. Instead of doing nothing or taking action that only makes the problem worse, common sense tells you to eliminate corrosive or dangerous elements before their destructive potential can spread. Yet sometimes people criticize God's commands to completely exterminate the people living in Canaan. They think it cruel of God to instruct the Israelites to wipe out everyone—men, women, and children.

But God saw the Canaanites in the same way we see a cavity in a tooth. God knew that if the corrosive influence wasn't removed, the whole nation of Israel could be weakened and eventually destroyed. These weren't harmless, innocent people the Israelites were routing. They worshiped false gods. Many of their religions involved sexual activity with shrine prostitutes. Some sacrificed their own children to their gods.

The Lord knew that if *all* these influences weren't removed, even the few that remained could have the same effect as one moldy orange at the bottom of a pile of good ones. Eventually the whole bunch would be ruined. That's why the tribes of Israel received such specific commands to run out all the people in the land of Canaan. Even though the land had been divided and the property lines drawn, there were still Canaanites within each tribe's boundaries who needed to be removed.

JOURNEY ONWARD

But if you read Judges 1, you will soon see that the tribes of Israel didn't heed Joshua's warning to drive out the Canaanites. Tribe after tribe failed to rid the land of its native inhabitants (Judges 1:19-36). Joshua had told the Israelites that if they failed to drive back the people of Canaan, then those people would become "snares and traps for you, whips on your backs and thorns in your eyes" (Joshua 23:13). Now, in Judges, God tells the Israelites the same thing (Judges 2:3). What happened as a result of the Israelites' failure to rid the land of the Canaanites? (Judges 2:10-15; 3:5-6)

God still loved His people, and wanted them to know that He was still in control of their lives. How did God lead the Israelites during this period, and how did the people respond? (2:16-19)

When the Israelites began to worship the Canaanite gods, the Lord allowed them to be conquered for eight years. Then He selected a judge to lead the people to victory. What was his name, and who was his famous relative? (3:7-10)

After 40 years of peace, the Israelites returned to idol worship, so God allowed them to go into captivity for another 18 years. They finally repented and God sent them a second judge. What was his name, and what was distinctive about him? (3:12-15)

How did this judge deliver Israel? (3:16-30)

This time the land of Israel had peace for 80 years. We don't know too much about the third judge. All we know is that his name was Shamgar and that he killed 600 Philistines with an oxgoad (a long stick used to drive animals). But even that little bit of information suggests that he must have been quite a guy. And he too saved Israel.

But soon the Israelites went back to their evil practices. God allowed them to be defeated again, this time for 20 years. The commander of the Canaanite army reigning over them was named Sisera, a cruel man who had 900 iron chariots at his command. The Israelites again cried out to God for help, and He sent a new judge. What was this judge's name and occupation? (4:4-7)

Deborah received word from God that a man named Barak should go fight Sisera. She volunteered to decoy Sisera into Barak's hands. But Barak didn't seem to have Deborah's courage. He said something like, "I'm not going without you" (4:8). Because of Barak's less than enthusiastic answer, Deborah told him he had lost the opportunity to be the real hero of the battle. That distinction would instead go to a woman.

The battle lines were drawn, the Israelites were victorious, and every man in Sisera's army was killed (4:16). However, Sisera escaped (which gave God the opportunity to fulfill Deborah's prophecy to Barak). How did her prediction come true? (4:17-24)

■

Deborah and Barak sang a song of praise to God, after which the land had peace for 40 years (Judges 5). Then guess what happened after that? You're right—the Israelites went right back to their old (evil) ways. And God again allowed them to go into captivity—this time at the hands of the Midianites. The Midianites were numerous and intensely oppressive to the Israelites, and the Israelites again repented of their sinful ways and turned back to God. So the Lord called a new person as judge. What was this judge's name, and what was he doing when God's messenger gave him the "good" news? (6:11)

■

How did the heavenly messenger address this person, and what was the message? (6:12)

■

Gideon was confused about God's will for the Israelites. He wanted to know why, since God had delivered the Israelites from the Egyptians, He had now "abandoned" them to the bondage of the Midianites. But the angel explained that it was going to be up to Gideon to change all that. Was Gideon confident in his ability to deliver Israel? Why? (6:15)

■

Gideon wanted a sign from God before he went any further, so he asked God to wait until he could gather together an offering. He offered a goat and some unleavened bread under the oak tree where the angel was waiting. What happened to the offering? (6:20-24)

After Gideon's visitor proved unmistakably that He spoke for God, He gave Gideon a job to do. God told Gideon to tear down some of the altars to foreign gods that were located in his neighborhood. (Some even belonged to Gideon's father.) Then he was to offer a bull to God as a burnt offering. Gideon was scared and waited until he had the cover of nightfall, but he still obeyed. When the townspeople discovered their idols destroyed, they wanted to kill him. But Gideon's father came up with a pretty good argument to defend his son. What did he tell his fellow townspeople? (6:30-32)

Since Gideon proved himself by passing this initial test, God gave him additional power—and a larger crisis to handle. Many of the Canaanite tribes were uniting with the Midianites and gathering against Israel. Gideon was still reluctant to accept the challenge without some kind of sign that God would get him through it. So he asked God (two different times) for a sign to show His support. What happened each time? (6:36-40)

After Gideon received assurance that God was truly behind him, he gathered his army together. But God told Gideon that he had too many men. God wanted the credit for victory over the Midianites to go to Him—not a large Israelite army. What was the first step Gideon took in reducing the size of his army? (7:1-3)

The number of enlisted fighting men was immediately reduced from 32,000 to 10,000 after that first step, but God said the army was still too large. What was the second step taken to reduce the size of the army? (7:4-8)

After taking that second step, the army was reduced from 10,000 to how many?

By this time the Lord must have expected Gideon to ask for a sign before leading his tiny army against the massive Midianite army. But before Gideon could ask, God told him to sneak down to the Midianite camp and keep his ears open. What did Gideon overhear? (7:9-15)

Gideon returned to his own camp full of confidence. And he had developed a unique battle plan to defeat the Midianites. What was his strategy? (7:16-20)

How did the plan work? (7:21-22)

As the Midianites were retreating, Gideon sent messengers to the territory of Ephraim for the men to come out and "head them off at the pass," so to speak. The Ephraimites were glad to help. But even before the battle had ended, they were complaining to Gideon that he hadn't let them join the fighting. Instead of arguing back or trying to defend himself, Gideon just explained that what the Ephraimites had done was every bit as important as what his army had done (8:1-3). The men of Ephraim were satisfied with Gideon's answer, but the incident shows why God had reduced the size of the Israelite army to begin with. The men of Israel were too quick to take credit for what *God* was doing for them.

While Gideon's 300 men went chasing after the retreating Midianites, their pursuit made them very tired and hungry. Gideon stopped at two different cities (Succoth and Peniel) and asked for food for his army, but both cities refused his request. He didn't have time to argue, and continued his pursuit of the Midianites. But after defeating their entire army, Gideon returned home by way of Succoth and Peniel. What did he do in each town? (8:16-17)

After the battle, the Israelites wanted Gideon and his family to rule over them. Gideon showed humility by refusing the offer and telling the people that God was their ruler—not any human leader. But immediately after his apparently wise decision, Gideon did something that wasn't so wise. What did he do, and what were the results of his actions? (8:22-27)

(NOTE: The word *ephod* often refers to the garment worn by the priests. But in this case, an ephod is an object created to be worshiped like an idol.)

During the rest of Gideon's life, the Israelites enjoyed 40 years of peace. Gideon had many wives and 70 sons in addition to a boy named Abimelech, born to him by a concubine. But as soon as Gideon died, the Israelites went right back to Baal worship.

A SELF-SERVING LEADER

In the previous instances, God had allowed the Israelites to be conquered and then had called a judge to deliver them. But after Gideon died, his successor was self-appointed. And this time the ungodly condition of the Israelites was reflected in the leadership of the nation.

Even though Gideon had 70 sons by legitimate wives, Abimelech (his child by a concubine) plotted to take Gideon's place as Israel's leader. Abimelech went first to his own relatives for support. They gave him money from one of the temples of Baal with which he recruited a band of men to fight for him. The men's first assignment was to execute the 70 real sons of Gideon. Abimelech's men accomplished their task with the exception of Gideon's youngest son, Jotham, who escaped.

On the day of Abimelech's "coronation," Jotham stood on a hillside overlooking the ceremony. He told the people a parable and then escaped again. Read the parable and write down what you think Jotham was trying to tell the people (9:7-20).

Abimelech governed the people for three years, after which God sent opposition to his leadership. A man named Gaal began to publicly criticize Abimelech, and Abimelech made plans to defeat Gaal and his followers. Abimelech won the preliminary battle and decided to pursue the fleeing rebels. He defeated one city, and the survivors barricaded themselves in a nearby tower. What did Abimelech do then? (9:46-49)

The strategy worked so well that Abimelech tried it again in the next city. But his plans didn't work so well this time. What happened? (9:50-53)

After getting injured, what did Abimelech do? (9:54-55)

Judges 9:56 tells us that God (the true leader of Israel) was responsible for the downfall of Abimelech (the self-appointed leader). Abimelech thought he had succeeded in his rebellion, but God didn't let his sin go unpunished. And after three years, Jotham's prediction came true.

After Abimelech's downfall, Israel was led for 23 years by a judge named Tola and then for 22 years by a judge named Jair. The appointments of these men are recorded in Judges 10:1-5, but not much is said about either one.

After Tola and Jair died, the Israelites' same bad patterns emerged. By this time they were worshiping any gods they could find—gods of the Moabites, the Ammonites, the Philistines, and more. The Lord allowed the Ammonites to overcome the Israelites. When the Israelites called out to Him for help, He told them to let their other gods deliver them. But the people confessed their sin and honestly repented, and God "could bear Israel's misery no longer" (10:16).

In the meantime, a guy named Jephthah was having personal problems. His professional reputation as a fighter was good, but his family reputation wasn't. His mother was a prostitute, which caused friction between Jephthah and his half brothers (the legitimate sons of his father). The legitimate sons determined that Jephthah wasn't going to get any of their father's inheritance, so they forced Jephthah to move to a neighboring land. There a group of followers gathered around him and he prospered as a mighty warrior.

That's about the time the Ammonites decided to gather against Israel. With no good prospects for leadership, a delegation from Israel went to see if Jephthah was willing to lead the Israelites. He agreed on one condition. What was it? (11:7-11)

Jephthah showed a lot of wisdom. Even though he had a widespread reputation as a good fighter, he began his dealings with the Ammonites by sending a letter asking exactly what they had against Israel. The Ammonite king replied that Israel had taken possession of some of the Ammonite land as they left Egypt, and he wanted to get it back. Jephthah replied that the Israelites had been forced to fight for the land, and that they had won it in the battle. But the Ammonite king wouldn't come to terms with Jephthah, and the two armies prepared for war.

Before going to battle with the Ammonites, Jephthah made a vow to the Lord. He promised that if God would help him win, he would offer to God the first thing that came out of his house when he got home. The Israelites defeated the Ammonites. But when Jephthah got home, what problem did he have honoring his vow to God? (11:32-40)

The passage you just read causes debate among Bible scholars as to whether Jephthah actually had his daughter killed. One side says that a vow to God would never be broken (Numbers 30:2). The other side says that Jephthah was knowledgeable about Israelite history and culture, based on his letter to the Ammonite king (Judges 11:14-27). Such a man, according to this group of people, would have known that God allowed a monetary atonement in certain cases in place of a blood sacrifice (Leviticus 27:1-8). This group believes that Jephthah paid the atonement price and "sacrificed" his daughter by dedicating her to God and never allowing her to marry. Both of these arguments are suppositions, and no one can say for sure what really happened.

Jephthah had problems with the Ephraimites much like those Gideon had faced. After the battle with the Ammonites, the men from Ephraim were angry that they had not been called into the battle. They ended up fighting Jephthah's men, but were defeated. Forty-two thousand of them died (Judges 12:1-6).

Jephthah led Israel for six years before he died. He was followed by three judges about whom little is known. Who were the three judges, and how long did each person rule? (12:8-15)

By now you know what happened after these judges died. The Israelites again rejected God's laws and did evil. This time their attackers were the Philistines and their bondage was 40 years. But God was preparing a special person to deliver the Israelites from the Philistines. The next session will examine the life of that special person, but here are some clues until then. You've no doubt heard of him, his hairstyle would have been popular in the 1960s, and no one would dare call him a wimp. If you need more clues, you may peek ahead to the next session, but be sure to come back and finish this one.

 JOURNEY INWARD

It's time for a self-examination on the topic of **self-concern.** A verse that perfectly sums up the attitude of the Israelites during the period of the judges is the last verse of the book: "In those days Israel had no king; everyone did as he saw fit" (Judges 21:25). Do you know people who don't really care about anyone except themselves? If so, how would you describe them?

By putting too much emphasis on self, one of two things usually happens. The first extreme is to get puffed up with pride about how much better you are than everyone else. The other extreme is to see all of your faults and shortcomings and decide you are worthless.

It's hard for people in either group to relate to God. Those in the first group just do whatever is convenient for *them.* God might interfere with their plans, so they find available, nonthreatening substitutes. That's what the Israelites did. They discovered they could worship the Canaanite gods without any major effect on their lifestyles. Only when God sent them the "inconvenience" of captivity did they repent.

The people God selected as deliverers were often in the second category. Many were reluctant heroes. But God can use any "nobody" who is willing to set aside his or her self-pity and feelings of worthlessness. He used two women (Deborah and Jael) to defeat one of the most cunning and battle-ready leaders of the Canaanites. (By the way, pitching tents was considered "women's work" in Israel, so Jael killed Sisera by using one of her everyday, ordinary talents for God.) Gideon was so afraid of the Midianites that he was hiding in a winepress to thresh his wheat without having it stolen by them. Jephthah came from the "wrong" kind of family. But God used all of these people who were willing to overcome *their* failures in order to accomplish *His* victories.

How about your life? What sins are you stubbornly clinging to that prevent a growing, maturing relationship with God?

Which of the judges in this session do you relate to most? Why?

 SNAPSHOTS

Era of Judges: Because the Israelites did not rid Canaan of all its inhabitants, they became corrupt and worshiped the false gods of the land. God raised up judges who would restore the land to peace.

Key Verse: "Unlike their fathers, they quickly turned from the way in which their fathers had walked, the way of obedience to the Lord's commands. Whenever the Lord raised up a judge for them, He was with the judge and saved them out of the hands of their enemies as long as the judge lived" (Judges 2:17-18).

Etc.: (Your own questions, comments, observations)

A WEAK STRONG MAN AND A STRONG WEAK WOMAN

(Judges 13–21; Book of Ruth)

If someone gave you a choice between love or power, which would you choose? To be more specific, if you could have either (A) or (B) below, which would be your choice?

(A) You may have the power to do whatever *you* want to do. No one can boss you around—not parents, not city officials, not *anybody*. You date whomever you want to date. You go where you want to go. You stay out as late as you want. And oh yeah, you're also well-built and strong. If anyone tries to stop you from getting what you want, you can overpower them with no problem.

(B) You may be involved in a loving relationship. It doesn't matter if you're dating anyone or not, because this kind of love is stronger than the boyfriend/girlfriend stuff that you're used to. But love isn't really love unless it is sacrificial, so you'll have to give up some (perhaps many) of the things that *you* want in order to please the other person. You have no guarantees that this loving relationship will last forever—or even until next week. But while the relationship exists, you will be loved and respected just because you are who you are.

Hopefully you gave your decision some serious thought, because it isn't an easy choice. Sociologist Tony Campolo says that love and power cannot coexist (*The Power Delusion,* Victor Books). If you desire power over someone, you do not truly love that person. And if you have established a truly loving relationship with someone, the desire for power will have faded. So at some point in your life, you *will* have to make the choice between power and love. In this session, you will examine the lives of a couple of people. One chose power over love, and the other opted for love no matter what.

JOURNEY ONWARD

First the power person. You received some clues to his identity at the end of the last session, and if you haven't guessed who it is yet, here are a few more hints. His father's name was Manoah. He was the first child of a woman who had previously been sterile. An angel appeared to the parents prior to the child's birth and told them he was to be a Nazirite, set apart for God, who would use him to deliver the Israelites from the Philistines. If you need any further help, the person's name is first mentioned in Judges 13:24.

[NOTE: Nazirites were consecrated to God and vowed not to drink alcoholic beverages, go near dead bodies, or cut their hair (Numbers 6:2-6). This was a lifelong commitment for Samson.]

How did the angel prove to Manoah that he was from God? (13:17-20)

How did Manoah and his wife respond to the angel's news? (13:21-23)

The Spirit of the Lord empowered Samson to begin to deliver Israel, and the Lord blessed him (13:24-25). The next we hear of Samson, he is ready to get married. But his parents objected. Why? (14:1-4)

Samson was taking his parents to meet his girlfriend when he was attacked by a lion. (He must have been walking ahead, or they were, because his parents didn't know of the attack.) What happened? (14:5-6)

Sometime later Samson saw the body of the lion again. What was different about it this time? (14:8-9)

As preparations were made for the wedding, Samson was given 30 groomsmen. He decided to use the story of the lion to create a riddle, and he bet his groomsmen a set of clothes apiece that they couldn't figure out his riddle before the wedding (a week later): "Out of the eater, something to eat; out of the strong, something sweet" (14:14). How did they finally come up with the right answer? (14:15-17)

What did Samson do when he discovered that the groomsmen had guessed the answer to his riddle? (14:18-19)

Since Samson wasn't present at his own wedding, what happened to the girl he was supposed to marry? (14:20)

Ⅰ

After Samson had time to cool off, he returned to his fiancée's house with a gift, but her father wouldn't let him in. The father explained that he thought Samson hated his daughter, so she had been given to another man to marry. The father offered Samson the girl's younger sister as a bride, but Samson declined the offer. What did he do instead? (15:1-5)

Ⅰ

How did the Philistines react to Samson's actions, and how did Samson retaliate? (15:6-8)

Ⅰ

Samson's revenge left the next step up to the Philistines, so they sent a delegation to the men of Judah and asked them to turn Samson in. Apparently the men of Judah were well aware of Samson's strength, because they sent 3,000 men to get him. And even then, they didn't try to take him without his permission. After Samson made them promise to take him to the Philistines and not to kill him themselves, he let the men of Judah tie him up with new ropes. Just as they reached the Philistines and started to give Samson to them, what happened? (15:14-19)

Ⅰ

The Philistines kept looking for good opportunities to capture Samson, and soon they had another chance. Describe the circumstances of the Philistine plot and of Samson's escape (16:1-3).

Ⅰ

But in spite of Samson's abundant strength, he had exposed a real weakness—Philistine women. The Philistines waited until he became fond of another woman and then bribed her to help them discover the secret of Samson's strength. The woman's name, of course, was Delilah. But she soon discovered that Samson wasn't willing to share his secret with her. When she asked what made him so strong, he gave her three false answers. What were the "secrets" he made up to keep from telling her the truth? (16:6-14)

How did Delilah finally convince Samson to confide in her? (16:15-16)

What was the result of Samson's true confession? (16:17-22)

Samson's capture was the source of much celebration and Dagon worship among the Philistines. They humiliated Samson by bringing him out to perform for the Philistine crowds. Apparently Samson had thought about his relationship with God, because he decided to pray. But even then, his prayer was rather self-centered. He wanted revenge on the Philistines because of what they had done to him. Yet God answered his prayer anyway. What was the result of Samson's prayer? (16:26-30)

THEY DID AS THEY SAW FIT

The Book of Judges is a depressing portion of the Old Testament. The great stories of its many heroes and heroines are overshadowed by a prevailing attitude of selfishness and complete disregard for God. And if the chapters we've covered so far (1–16) aren't bad enough, the final chapters (17–21) contain an assortment of stories that further emphasize Israel's state of spiritual decay during this time. The glory days of Joshua were quickly forgotten as the Israelites blotted out of their minds the great things God had done for them.

For instance, Judges 17–18 records the story of a man named Micah. He had formed for himself an assortment of idols, a shrine, and some other worship articles. He then met a Levite from the tribe of Judah and hired him to be his personal priest.

In the meantime, the tribe of Dan had been unable to run the Canaanites out of the land they were supposed to inherit and were looking around for a place to live. They happened to find out about the priest who was living at Micah's house, so they offered to hire him away from Micah. The Levite accepted the Danites' offer and went with them, taking Micah's idols as he left. Then the tribe of Dan attacked a peaceful, unsuspecting people, took their city, renamed it Dan, and made it a center of idol worship.

Another graphic example of the rock-bottom spiritual condition of the Israelites follows in Judges 19–21. A man was traveling with his concubine and a young male servant. He refused to stay in an alien city and insisted on moving to Gibeah, a city of Israel—where he assumed he would be much safer. They sat in the town square for a long time without anyone inviting them to stay (which should have been the custom). Finally, an old man saw them sitting there and insisted that they come home with him. His was something of an ominous invitation. What happened at the man's house that night? (19:20-26)

The next morning the man's concubine was dead. What did the man do with her? (19:27-30)

The unrestrained cruelty of the men of Gibeah was too much for the other Israelites—even in their unspiritual condition. When they heard what had happened in Gibeah (a city in Benjamin), they united to fight the Benjamites. They first gave the men of Gibeah a chance to turn over the guilty people so they alone could be punished. But the Benjamites refused and put together their own army. In the battle that followed, casualties were heavy on both sides, but the Israelites finally defeated the Benjamites. In fact, only 600 Benjamite men remained after the battle, and the tribe almost became extinct. But the rest of the Israelites had compassion on the remaining men of Benjamin and helped them find wives to rebuild their tribe.

Both of these stories at the end of the Book of Judges reflect the absence of any spiritual standards among God's people. It was a time of "free-lance" priests, entire cities eager to indulge in homosexuality and rape, savage attitudes, and an absolute refusal to repent of sin. Yet with these stories and the observation that "in those days . . . everyone did as he saw fit" (21:25), the Book of Judges ends.

REDEEMING LOVE

But the Book of Ruth that immediately follows gives quite a different picture of humanity. The first verse of Ruth tells us that the story takes place "in the days when the judges ruled." It also tells of a famine that is not mentioned in the Book of Judges.

The story of Ruth begins as a man named Elimelech from Bethlehem (in the tribe of Judah) takes his wife (Naomi) and two sons (Mahlon and Kilion) to Moab to escape the famine. In Moab, the two sons married native women named Orpah and Ruth. The names may be confusing, but half the characters drop out of the story right away. What happened to them? (Ruth 1:3-4)

Naomi received word that the famine in Israel was over, and she prepared to return home. She told Ruth and Orpah to go back to their original homes in Moab. They were torn between their desire to remain in their own country and their friendship with Naomi. What did they eventually decide to do? (1:8-18)

It wasn't easy for Naomi to return to Bethlehem and pick up her life without her husband and with a foreign daughter-in-law. But Ruth did everything she could to help Naomi. Ruth volunteered to go into the fields where they were harvesting grain and pick up whatever was left. Where did she go to glean? (2:3)

As the owner (Boaz) returned from a trip to the city, he quickly noticed the new girl who was following his men around and picking up whatever grain she could gather. What did he tell her? (2:8-9)

Ruth was amazed that this stranger would be so kind to her. He explained that he had heard about the many kind things she had been doing for her mother-in-law, Naomi. Then he gave her a blessing and something to eat. He didn't tell her that he was from the same clan as Elimelech, Naomi's husband. Then when Ruth left to glean some more, Boaz gave instructions to his men. What did he tell them? (2:14-16)

That evening as Ruth was feeding Naomi from the barley she had gleaned, Naomi was naturally eager to hear how Ruth's day had gone. When Ruth told her about this nice guy named Boaz, Naomi was amazed at the "coincidence" that Ruth had chosen the field of someone whom Naomi was related to. Naomi referred to Boaz as a *kinsman-redeemer,* a person responsible for taking care of family members who needed help. So Ruth was encouraged by both Boaz and Naomi to continue gleaning in Boaz's fields until the harvest was completed.

Not long afterward, Naomi decided she should help Ruth get "fixed up" with a husband. And she figured Boaz would make a nice husband for Ruth. What advice did Naomi give Ruth? (3:1-5)

Naomi's instructions may sound a little strange to us today. But in the custom of Israel, Ruth was asking Boaz for a marriage proposal. Boaz was overjoyed, but he had some bad news for her. What kept Boaz from marrying Ruth right away? (3:10-13)

Ruth slept at Boaz's feet and left in the morning before anyone knew she had been there. But her integrity cannot be questioned (3:11). Before she left, Boaz gave her grain from the threshing floor as a gift. When she got home, all she and Naomi could do was wait to see what would happen from Boaz's investigations.

When Boaz met with the other kinsman-redeemer, he first brought up the matter of a piece of land that Naomi was having to sell. The nearest kinsman-redeemer would be obligated to buy it for her. Was the other man willing to purchase it for Naomi? (4:3-4)

Then Boaz explained that there was a "string attached" to the purchase of the land. What did he tell the other kinsman-redeemer? (4:5)

And how did the other kinsman-redeemer respond? (4:6)

The other kinsman-redeemer gave Boaz one of his sandals to make the transaction official. (This was another Israelite custom.) Then Boaz made a public announcement that he intended to marry Ruth. And if this love story isn't significant enough, it is even more dramatic when you discover who was descended from Ruth and Boaz. Who was to become Ruth's noteworthy great-grandson? (4:13-17)

 JOURNEY INWARD

After examining the lives of Samson and Ruth, reconsider your answer to the opening illustration of this session concerning **love vs. power.** Do you want to change your answer? If not, do you have better reasons for sticking with your original answer?

If you had to identify one major weakness that led to Samson's downfall, what would you say it was?

It may be hard for a "normal" person to relate to Samson because of his tremendous strength. But consider that not even Samson's strength was sufficient to insure his success in life. Just think what kind of hero he would have been had he yielded to God's laws and disciplined himself mentally and morally. What are some problems in your life that you are trying to take care of on your own power? After each problem you list, determine how you can include God in your efforts to deal with it in the future.

Now consider Ruth's example of love. When she decided to leave her homeland and return to Israel with a moneyless mother-in-law she could hardly have known, she could expect no reward of any kind. Yet God blessed her, and her life couldn't have worked out better. Do you think Ruth is an exception, or do you think God eventually rewards *every* act of genuine love?

Complete the following chart by filling in five names (friends, family members, etc.) under each column.

PEOPLE I FIND EASY TO LOVE	PEOPLE I FIND SOMEWHAT HARD TO LOVE	PEOPLE I FIND HARD TO LOVE

Review all the names on your lists and determine to practice more love and less power the next time you see each of those people. (Of course, you'll probably have to try harder for the people in the last column.)

As you can see, you're almost through with this book. If you're working your way through the entire Old Testament, you only have three more books to go. If you're stopping with this book, hopefully you learned something about God *and* about yourself during the past few weeks.

One suggestion: If you do plan to continue with this series, be sure you have completed this book first. It puts the next one in perspective. The second book in this series will cover the era of the Israelite kings. And you won't want to miss those stories: Saul, David, Solomon, Elijah, Elisha, the notorious Ahab and Jezebel. Slingshots fell giants. Fire falls from heaven. Wicked people are eaten by dogs. And again, a few of God's people stand out against mass wickedness.

If you don't mind, please take two more minutes to complete the form on page 155. We want to know how you're responding to the books in this series so we can be sure we're staying on target. Your help is greatly appreciated.

 SNAPSHOTS

Samson: The Lord raised up Samson to begin the deliverance of the Israelites from their Philistine oppression. He was empowered by God with extraordinary strength.

Ruth: Ruth, the Moabite widow of an Israelite, followed her mother-in-law back to Israel. Boaz, a kinsman-redeemer, married Ruth.

Key Verse: "Where you go I will go, and where you stay I will stay. Your people will be my people and your God my God" (Ruth 1:16).

Etc.:   (Your own questions, comments, observations)

THE SAGA BEGINS
BibleLog Book 1

Please help us by taking a few moments to give us your honest feedback on this book. Your opinion is appreciated!

WHAT DID YOU THINK?

Did you enjoy this book? Why or why not?

How has this book helped you . . .
- understand the Bible better?

- apply the Bible to your life?

Have you used other books in this series? If so, which ones?

Do you plan to continue this series?

In what setting did you use this elective? (circle one)

Sunday School   Youth group   Midweek Bible study   On your own

Other _____

About how long did it take to work through each session?

Did you complete the studies on your own before discussing them with a group? (circle one)

Always   Usually   Sometimes   Rarely   Never   Did them as a group

Other _____

What grade are you in?

(Optional)

Name _____

Address _____

Additional comments:

SonPower Youth Sources Editor
1825 College Avenue
Wheaton, Illinois 60187